KISS CHASE
AND
CONKERS

Chambers

CAROLINE SANDERSON

KISS CHASE
AND
CONKERS
The Games We Played

Chambers

CHAMBERS
An imprint of Chambers Harrap Publishers Ltd
7 Hopetoun Crescent, Edinburgh, EH7 4AY

Chambers Harrap is an Hachette Livre UK company

© Chambers Harrap Publishers Ltd 2008

Chambers® is a registered trademark of Chambers Harrap Publishers Ltd

First published by Chambers Harrap Publishers Ltd 2008

Database right Chambers Harrap Publishers Ltd (makers)

A CIP catalogue record for this book is available from the British Library.

ISBN 978 0550 10427 4

10 9 8 7 6 5 4 3 2 1

www.chambers.co.uk

Extracts p33, p127, pp186–7 from p7, p169, pp15–16 of *Children's Games in Street and Playground* by Iona and Peter Opie (Oxford at the Clarendon Press, 1969) © Iona and Peter Opie.

Contributors:
Project Manager, Editor and Picture Researcher: Hilary Marsden
Prepress: Andrew Butterworth
Publishing Manager: Hazel Norris

Designed by Chambers Harrap Publishers Ltd, Edinburgh
Typeset in Miller Text by Chambers Harrap Publishers Ltd, Edinburgh
Printed and bound in Great Britain by MPG Books Ltd, Bodmin, Cornwall

Contents

Contents

Contents

Introduction

'What games did you play when you were young?'

Whatever their age, most people love to reminisce about the playtimes of their childhood, those blissful days before the cares of adult life took the shine off the untrammelled instinct for fun and invention that inhabits every child.

Those of us currently bringing up our own children enjoy finding in their play echoes of our youth in the 1960s, 70s and 80s. Such days seem scarcely a moment ago, but were nevertheless lived out in markedly different times. And the grandparents and great-grandparents of today look back, often rather wistfully, on childhoods lent a decided austerity by the deprivations of the war and post-war years. By contrast, 21st-century children are growing up in a fast-paced consumer age, their very different childhoods a source of wonder and worry to those who remember 'how things used to be'.

Children today still love to play games, however. The proof is in any park or school playground. And in these days of credit crunch and climate change, when attention is turning once more to the homemade and to other economical ways of living, traditional games are an invaluable form of entertainment. In the spirit of ages both past and present, therefore, I would like to offer this book as an aid to making your own fun, however old or young you may be.

The games described here are, without exception, cheap and easy to play, and require a minimum of equipment and preparation. There are games for any circumstance in which you might find yourself: whether in a field with a ball and six unruly youngsters; faced with a roomful of bored relatives at Christmas; stuck in a school hall with a class of stir-crazy infants on a wet afternoon; or apprehensive at hosting a children's birthday party with two whole hours to fill.

Introduction

There are perennial favourites that will be familiar to all and need little introduction, although their history and variants may hold a few surprises. Other games will be unknown to the children of today but will evoke in older readers memories of times past. A revival of many of the games enjoyed by earlier generations is long overdue.

From Kiss Chase to Conkers, games have always been part of human existence, providing ritual, exercise, behavioural training for adulthood, healthy competition and, in some cases, a very good imitation of life itself. They are also jolly good fun. Remember how to play games and you remember how to enjoy yourself. What could be better therapy for young or old?

Caroline Sanderson
July 2008

What games did *you* play when you were young? The publishers warmly welcome all comments, suggestions and recollections from members of the public, which will be considered for incorporation in future editions. Please send your suggestions for regional variations, overlooked classics or personal favourites to: The Editor, *Kiss Chase and Conkers*, Chambers Harrap Publishers Ltd, 7 Hopetoun Crescent, Edinburgh EH7 4AY.

About the Author

Caroline Sanderson is a writer whose articles and reviews have appeared in *The Times, Mslexia, Child Education* and *The Bookseller*, for which she writes a monthly column previewing non-fiction. She is the author of a children's book, *Pick Your Brains: Greece,* and a travel book for adults, *A Rambling Fancy: In the Footsteps of Jane Austen.* Married with two children, Caroline lives in Gloucestershire, where she plays games as often as she can.

Acknowledgements

Anyone who undertakes even the most superficial research into children's games soon finds themselves indebted to the work of Iona and Peter Opie, and especially their *Children's Games in Street and Playground.* I am no exception and gratefully acknowledge this invaluable resource.

I would like to thank: Hilary Marsden and Sarah Such for all their help; Olivia and Florence Hinkley for sharing their clapping rhymes, tag games and much more; Peter and Margaret Sanderson and Jill and Barney Stanley for their memories of 'during the war'; the children of Rodborough Community Primary School for letting me stand in the playground and watch; and most of all my own children, Alexander and Julia Brookes, for playing games with me.

The publishers would like to thank Ellie and Jamie Westhead for their cheerful demonstration of some of these games for the camera, and Eva White who 'loves butter'. They would also like to thank all those who suggested games for inclusion.

Image Credits

Battleships, p7 © *Hazel Norris*; **Blind Man's Buff**, p11 © *Roger-Viollet / Topfoto*; **Blow Football**, p13 © *geogphotos / Alamy*; **The Bumps**, p19 © *Hulton-Deutsch Collection / Corbis*; **The Buttercup Game**, p21 © *Patrick White*; **The Mother of Invention**, p25 © *TopFoto*; **Cat's Cradle**, pp28–31 © *Hazel Norris*; **Amusements of the Ancients**, p32 © *Mary Evans Picture Library / Alamy*; **Charades**, pp35–7 © *Hazel Norris*; **Chinese Whispers**, p39 © *Hazel Norris*; **Cigarette-card Skimming**, pp40–1 © *Roger Mayne / Mary Evans Picture Library*; **Clapping Games**, p45 © *digitalskillet / iStockphoto.com*, pp46–7 © *Hazel Norris*; **Conkers**, pp48–9 © *Jenny Matthews / Alamy*, p50 © *Krzyszt / Gorski / iStockphoto.com*; **Consequences**, p54 © *Hazel Norris*; **Brueghel's Children**, p57 © *The London Art Archive / Alamy*; **Cops and Robbers**, p58 © *The Scotsman Publications Ltd. Licensor www.scran.ac.uk*; **Follow My Leader**, pp70–1 © *Ken Russell / TopFoto*; **French Cricket**, p73 © *Topfoto / PA*; **French Skipping**, p75 © *plainpicture GmbH & Co. KG / Alamy*, pp76–7 © *Hazel Norris*; **Grandmother's Footsteps**, p79 © *Lisa Payne / Alamy*; **Hand Shadows**, pp81–2 © *compucow / iStockphoto.com*; **Hangman**, p83 © *Hazel Norris*; **The Hat Game**, p85 © *Hazel Norris*; **Headstands and Handstands, Cartwheels and Crabs**, p89 © *Hazel Norris*, p90 © *Janine Wiedel Photolibrary / Alamy*; **Here We Go Round the Mulberry Bush**, pp92–3 © *Mary Evans Picture Library / Alamy*; **Hide and Seek**, p95 © *Time & Life Pictures / Getty Images*; **Hopscotch**, p99 © *Caro / TopFoto*; **Hunt the Slipper**, p103 © *Mary Evans Picture Library / Alamy*; **Husky Bum**, p106 © *Haywood Magee / Hulton Archive / Getty Images*; **I Spy**, p111 © *Antiques & Collectables / Alamy*; **Jacks**, p112 © *Christine Glade / iStockphoto.com*, p114 © *oneclearvision / iStockphoto.com*; **The Novelist at Play**, p116 © *Mary Evans Picture Library / Alamy*; **Kim's Game**, p121 © *Hazel Norris*; **Revival Meeting?**, p125 © *Julie de Leseleuc / iStockphoto.com*; **Kiss Chase**, p126 © *Clare Charleson / Alamy*; **Knock Down Ginger**, p129 © *Bubbles Photolibrary / Alamy*; **Leapfrog**, pp134–5 © *Hazel Norris*; **Amusing 'The Youth of Great Britain'**, p137 © *Mary Evans Picture Library*; **Marbles**, p138 © *Ron Bailey / iStockphoto.com*, p141 © *Newsquest (Herald & Times). Licensor www.scran.ac.uk*, p142 © *Hazel Norris*; **Murder in the Dark**, p145 © *Hazel Norris*; **North of the Border**, p147 © *Bert Hardy / Hulton Archive / Getty Images*; **Musical Chairs**, p149 © *Richard Kolker / Photonica / Getty Images*; **Noughts and Crosses**, p151 © *Hazel Norris*; **Come into My Parlour**, p154 © *Amoret Turner / Alamy*; **In the Land of Bards**, p163 © *Robin Weaver / Alamy*; **Oranges and Lemons**, p165 © *ClassicStock / TopFoto*; **Pass the Balloon**, p168 © *Anja Frers / Photonica / Getty Images*; **Let's Pretend**, p170 © *Bubbles Photolibrary / Alamy*; **Pass the Parcel**, pp172–3 © *Bubbles Photolibrary / Alamy*; **Piggy in the Middle**, p175 © *TopFoto*; **Pin the Tail on the Donkey**, p177 © *Nina Shannon / iStockphoto.com*, p178 © *ClassicStock / TopFoto*; **Poohsticks**, p182 © *Robert Judges / Alamy*; **Playing Out**, p186 © *TopFoto*, p187 © *TopFoto*; **Queenie**, p192 © *Mary Evans Picture Library*; **Ring a Ring of Roses**, p195 © *Lisa Payne / Alamy*; **Sign Here**, p199 *Privately owned image, reproduced by permission of Rita Marsden*; **Rounders**, p201 © *Ace Stock Limited / Alamy*; **Skipping Games**, p205 © *Andrzej Tokarski / iStockphoto.com*, p206 © *TopFoto*, p208 © *Tamara Peel / iStockphoto.com*; **Spillikins**, p211 © *babylee / iStockphoto.com*; **Stone, Paper, Scissors**, pp212–14 © *NickyBlade / iStockphoto.com*; **Stone Skimming**, p215 © *Richard Osbourne / Blue Pearl Photographic / Alamy*; **Tag**, pp218–19 © *ImageWorks / TopFoto*; **Many Happy Returns**, p220 © *TopFoto*; **Three-legged Race**, p222 © *Scottish Mining Museum. Licensor www.scran.ac.uk*; **Tiddlywinks**, p224 © *The National Trust Photolibrary / Alamy*, p225 © *The Scotsman Publications Ltd. Licensor www.scran.ac.uk*; **Tin Can Tommy**, p227 © *Birgid Allig / zefa / Corbis*; **Traffic Lights**, p232 © *Sabrina dei Nobili / iStockphoto.com*; **Plus Ça Change ...**, p236 © *Sally and Richard Greenhill / Alamy*; **Wheelbarrow Race**, p239 © *Scottish Mining Museum. Licensor www.scran.ac.uk*; **Wink Murder**, p240 © *Hazel Norris*; **Playground Crazes**, p243 © *TopFoto*; **Yellow Car**, pp244–5 © *Brett Hillyard / iStockphoto.com*

Cover image © *Time & Life Pictures / Getty Images*

Author photo © *Dan Wootton*

Games

Alphabet Games
Not As Easy As A, B, C

There are many alphabet games. Although a little redolent of the swot, they do boost word power and sometimes general knowledge, not to mention the memory. The more popular ones include the following.

The School Teacher
One player is chosen to be the School Teacher. The other players sit in a circle with the Teacher in the middle. The Teacher chooses a category, and asks one of the players to name something belonging to the category that begins with a certain letter. So if the category is 'birds', the Teacher might ask for a bird beginning with P. And the player might reply 'peacock' or 'pigeon' or 'pheasant', and so on. If the player cannot come up with a bird within a certain time (about ten seconds), that player is out and the turn passes to the next player.

Alphabet Lists
Everyone is given a piece of paper with the letters of the alphabet written in order on it, one below the other – it might be kinder to leave out horrors such as Q, X and Z. A leader or adult chooses a category (for example towns in the UK) and everyone tries to write down a town beginning with each letter, within a set time. The person who completes the most letters is the winner.

Alphabet Places
Each letter of the alphabet is written on a slip of paper and the 26 slips are

placed in a hat. The players sit in a circle, and a letter is drawn at random from the hat. Everyone in the circle in turn names a place (which might be a country, a town, a river, etc) beginning with that letter. No repetition is permitted. Anyone who fails to come up with an answer loses a life. If players lose three lives, they are out. Once everyone has run out of ideas, a new round begins with a new letter.

The Minister's Cat

The players sit in a circle and the first player begins by saying 'The minister's cat is a ... cat', filling in the space with an adjective beginning with A, for example 'admirable'. The next player repeats the sentence, adding an adjective beginning with B, such as 'brave', so the sentence becomes 'The minister's cat is an admirable, brave cat'. The game continues until a player forgets a word (in which case they are out) or the alphabet is used up. The game can be made easier for younger children by omitting the repetition element so that only one adjective is used at a time, although the adjectives are still added in alphabetical order. The Minister's Cat is an ideal game for long car journeys.

Portmanteau

This variation on the Minister's Cat begins with the first player saying 'I went on holiday and with me I took a ... ', filling in the gap with an object beginning with A (for example 'an apple'). The next player must repeat the sentence and add an object

2

beginning with B, for example 'I went on holiday and with me I took an apple, and a blanket'. And play goes on until someone is out or the alphabet is used up. 'I went to the shop and I bought ...' is another popular version.

The Name Game

The first player says the name of a famous person, for example 'Marlon Brando'. The next player must then come up with another famous person whose first name begins with the same initial letter as the previous person's last name, for example 'Britney Spears'. First and last names which have the same initial letter – for example 'Brigitte Bardot' or 'Ronald Reagan' – reverse the order of play and mean that the person whose turn it was previously has to go again, keeping players on their toes. This is another good game to play in the car.

Spelling Bee

The simplest alphabet game of all players spell aloud words given to them by a referee. This can be played in teams, with each correct spelling being rewarded with a point. It is a good idea, though, to have a dictionary to hand in case of disputes, particularly if players are going to be asked to spell difficult words like 'antidisestablishmentarianism'!

Bad Egg

A Simply Cracking Game

One player (Bad Egg) takes a ball (a tennis ball is ideal) and stands with her back to the other players. She chooses a subject or category, for example flowers, colours or football teams. Each of the other players must then shout out a name for themselves from the chosen category, for example Rose, Daisy, Bluebell, Tulip, Daffodil or Buttercup.

Bad Egg chooses one of the names to call out – for instance, 'Daisy' – and at the same time throws the ball high into the air over her shoulder. 'Daisy' tries to catch the ball, while the other players scatter as far away as possible. When 'Daisy' retrieves the ball, she shouts 'Stop!' and all the players must immediately stay where they are. 'Daisy' can then take three paces towards any player and try to hit them below the knee with the ball. If she succeeds, the player who has been hit becomes Bad Egg. If she misses, she becomes Bad Egg.

In one variant, when the player who has caught the ball shouts 'Stop', the other players must stand with their legs apart. Instead of hitting another player below the knee, the player with the ball must roll it through their legs from where she is standing.

Bad Egg is a slightly more sophisticated version of 'Catch Ball', a game that dates at least from the early 19th century. In Catch Ball, the thrower of the ball calls out the name of the player he wishes to try to catch it. The chosen player must catch the ball before it has bounced twice on the ground. If he succeeds, he then throws the ball up for another nominated player. If he fails, he loses a point and someone else throws the ball. When a player has lost four points, he is out of the game, and has the ball thrown at his back by the others.

In 'Eggity-Budge', a game popular in Yorkshire in the 1950s, a player is chosen to be It. Another player throws the ball as far away as possible in any direction and It goes to retrieve it, while the other players run around. When It gets the ball, he shouts 'Eggity Budge' and all the other players stand still. Then It chooses a player to hit, and may take three hops, three steps and the distance of three spits on the ground towards them before attempting to strike them below the knee. If It succeeds, the player who has been hit is out of the game. If the ball misses, however, It must race after the ball again while everyone runs further away until the ball is retrieved and 'Eggity Budge' is called once more.

In all these versions, play continues until everyone gets bored, or is too tired to carry on!

Battleships
Hit and Miss

Battleships is an excellent pencil and paper game for two players. The preparation is easier if players can use the sort of squared paper printed in maths exercise books; otherwise, each player draws a grid, twelve squares by twelve on a piece of plain paper. Number the squares going across 1, 2, 3, etc, and letter the squares going down A, B, C, etc.

Keeping their grid hidden from their opponent, each player draws in the ships in their fleet. Traditionally, this consists of five or six ships of varying sizes; if players have sufficient naval knowledge, they can specify each kind of vessel. The squares occupied by each ship are shaded in or the lines that enclose them are thickened.

Possible fleet combinations include:

> 1 battleship (5 squares)
>
> 1 cruiser (4 squares)
>
> 2 destroyers (3 squares each)
>
> 1 submarine (1 square)
>
> 1 corvette (1 square)

or

> 1 aircraft carrier (5 squares)
>
> 1 battleship (4 squares)
>
> 1 destroyer (3 squares)
>
> 1 submarine (3 squares)
>
> 1 patrol boat (2 squares)

Players take it in turns to call out the number of a square –
for instance, 4D – and if that square coincides with any
part of one of their opponent's ships, the other player must
say 'hit'. A 'ship' is 'destroyed' if all the squares it occupies
are specified by the opposing player. Sound effects add to
the fun – a loud wail of descending pitch followed by either
a muted plop or, in the event of a hit, an explosive noise,
works well.

If a player scores a hit, he gets another go, and can attempt
to finish off the entire ship by choosing a square adjacent
to the hit and hoping that it scores a bullseye. When a ship
is sunk, the player on the receiving end of the attack must
announce it by saying, for instance, 'Battleship destroyed'.

If a player calls out a square that does not coincide with a
ship, it is pronounced a 'miss' and the other player takes
a turn. The first player to knock out his opponent's entire
fleet is the winner.

A good tip for avoiding confusion is for players to mark their grid with both the 'hits' scored by the other player (perhaps with an X) and the squares they have called out themselves (perhaps with a tick).

A more complex version of the game awards players as many attempts at a hit during their turn as the ships they still have in the game. So at the beginning, each player chooses five squares in each turn. Only at the end of each turn does the opponent announce which of the guesses are hits and which have missed. If a hit is scored, the opponent must also say which ship has been struck (or ships, if more than one has been hit), making it possible to determine the size of the beleaguered vessel before earmarking the next squares to attack.

Nowadays it is possible to buy ready-made pegboard games of Battleships, which remove the need for the humble pencil and paper. Video versions have also been produced for the various games consoles. But, like Hangman and Noughts and Crosses, the beauty of Battleships is that it can be played almost anywhere as long as paper and pen or pencil are to hand.

WIN OR LOSE
The Etiquette of Games

It does not matter how often adults impress upon them that it is the taking part that is important, children generally find the idea ridiculous; games are about winning or losing.

The competitive gene with which many children are endowed impels them to do everything possible to triumph over their fellow players. Whether they are playing Tag or Tiddlywinks, the will to win is so strong that even cheating is preferable to losing. The alternative is to accuse someone else of cheating. It is always worth a loud shout of 'That's not fair!' if things are not going to plan. The risk is that the whole game will descend into chaos, with players squaring up to one another, going off in a huff, or worse, in tears. And that is

If you can meet with Triumph and Disaster

And treat those two impostors just the same ...

Rudyard Kipling

the end of a game that was supposed to be fun.

Kipling's idea that one of the qualifications for being a man is the ability to handle triumph and disaster with equanimity is a difficult concept for most children to grasp. A win is not a win unless it is accompanied by an extravagant victory celebration and a certain amount of crowing over one's opponents: 'Losers! Losers!'. Losing means arguments, tears or sulks, or any combination of the three.

Good sportsmanship – that is, learning to both win and lose with good grace – is a very British idea, and one which parents have to work hard to instil in their children. Unfortunately, although their offspring may grow up having been taught to play fair, they encounter an adult world full of winners and losers. So children, arguably, have a much better grasp of the realities of life!

Blind Man's Buff
Touchy Feely Fun

Blind Man's Buff – a 'buff' being a small push – was a popular Victorian parlour game and is still enjoyed today.

One player, the Blind Man, has their eyes covered by a blindfold, usually a scarf tied behind their head. Someone turns the Blind Man round several times so that they lose all sense of direction, and then they must walk around the room, holding their hands out in front of them until they bump into another player. If the Blind Man manages to identify the caught player correctly from the feel of their face and clothes, the blindfold is removed and someone else has a turn. If the Blind Man fails to identify the other player, they remain blindfolded and try again.

In an easier version ideal for younger children, the Blind Man is allowed three guesses. Making the other players stand on the spot while the Blind Man roams around also makes things easier for little ones, although players are still allowed to duck and bend to avoid being touched. To make things more difficult, players can don funny hats, moustaches or even complete changes of clothes, in order to disguise their identities.

Blind Man's Buff can also be played as a version of Tag, in which the Blind Man attempts to 'tag' the other players without being able to see them, while the other players scatter to avoid being tagged, sometimes teasing the Blind Man to make him change direction. When the Blind Man succeeds in tagging another player, that player is out of the game, and play continues until everyone is eliminated. A new Blind Man is then blindfolded.

'Seated Blind Man's Buff' is an adult but enjoyably immature version of the game, in which players sit in a circle on chairs and the Blind Man sits on each lap in turn. The Blind Man must identify the owner of the lap without touching any other part of the body. Sounds made by the person being sat upon usually provide clues.

There is also an aquatic Blind Man's Buff known as 'Marco Polo', most often played in a swimming pool. Instead of a blindfold, the chasing player simply closes their eyes. To locate the other players the chasing player calls out 'Marco', whereupon all the others must reply 'Polo'.

Blind Man's Buff was known to the ancient Greeks, and has been widely played over the centuries. The game is even depicted in a beautiful painting by the 18th-century French artist Jean-Honoré Fragonard. In the USA the game is called 'Blind Man's Bluff', but more colourful alternative names are to be found in European countries; in Italy it is known as *mosca cieca* (meaning 'blind fly'); in Germany, *Blindekuh* ('blind cow'); and in Spain *gallina ciega* ('blind hen'). Most evocative of all is its French name, *colin-maillard,* which derives from a medieval fight between a lord from Louvain and a man named Colin who was armed with a mallet and who was blinded in the course of the battle. As with many games and rhymes, this gruesome origin would scarcely be suspected from the benign version that has come down to us.

Blow Football
Breathless Excitement

Blow Football is an uproarious indoor game for two or more players. Playing the game requires a table, a ping-pong ball and a drinking straw for each player (the bendy ones are ideal).

Players divide into two teams and stand at opposite ends of the table, with the ping-pong ball placed in the middle. On a signal (a whistle would be very appropriate), players try to blow the ball towards the opposing team's goal, ie the opposite end of the table. To score, a team must succeed in blowing the ball right over the edge of the table and onto the floor. If a goal is scored, the ball is replaced in the centre and the team that conceded the goal gets first blow. If the ball drops from the side of the table, it is not a goal, and play restarts with the ball placed back in the middle.

The only rule in Blow Football is that players are not allowed to touch the ball while it is in play, either with their straw, their hand or any other part of the body. If the ball is touched, the opposing team gets a penalty; the ball is placed in the middle of the pitch and they can blow the ball freely into the net while the penalized team watches.

To avoid chasing errant ping-pong balls all over the room, or to make the game harder, players can adopt the rule that the ball must drop into a container (a bucket or bowl placed at each end of the table) for the goal to count.

Commercial versions of Blow Football have been available since the early 20th century. These add such sophistications as actual goals and a proper playing pitch with raised boundaries. But most games are impromptu, and players improvise, with margarine tubs for goals and books placed around the edge of the table to stop the ball falling off.

Lung capacity is an important factor in Blow Football, and the main reason why older, unfit players can be found wanting at crucial moments. Anyone who starts hyperventilating should be ordered to sit on the touchline until they recover.

If a game of football does not appeal, the equipment can be adapted for a simple ping-pong race, in which players compete to blow the ball along a course and be first past the winning post.

Ping-pong balls have a remarkable propensity for getting lost, crushed, trodden on or carried off by over-enthusiastic dogs. Happily, Blow Football can also be played with dried peas or beans, or even with a temptingly edible item like a jelly bean or a certain brand of spherical chocolate with a light honeycomb centre. When such a ball is used, players have been known to use their own mouths to form the goals. This is not advisable; it is not only a choking hazard, but also a sure-fire way of getting through an unhealthy amount of chocolate!

British Bulldog

Bruises De Rigueur

Some of the more adrenaline-fuelled moments of many people's childhood were spent playing British Bulldog on the tarmac playground of their primary school. Why the game was not played on the softer grass surface of the playing fields is hard to explain; many an injury might have been avoided if it had. But such was the mania for this game among many children that the odd flesh wound did not seem to dampen it in the slightest.

The game begins with two safe areas being designated at either end of the 'pitch'. One person – the Bulldog or Catcher – stands in between the two safe areas. The object of the game is for players to run from one safe area to the opposite safe area without being intercepted by the Bulldog. To take a player captive, the Bulldog must grab them, lift them bodily off the ground and shout 'British Bulldog, one, two, three' before they can break free. If a player succeeds in getting away, they rejoin their team. If not, they too become a Bulldog. In the closing stages of the game, Bulldogs often outnumber the remaining runners, making for some very rough captures as a whole pack of Bulldogs attempts to rugby-tackle their prey. An additional hazard is created when two groups of children simultaneously attempt to bulldoze their way across the pitch in opposite directions. Head-on collisions are frequent, and it is no surprise that British Bulldog holds the dubious distinction of being probably the most-banned game of all time in British schools.

In some versions of British Bulldog, instead of the whole herd attempting to cross at once (it is common for a game to involve twenty children or more) one player is singled out to cross first, before the rest follow in the 'rush' or 'bullrush'. 'Tag Bullrush' is a less violent version in which you only need to be tagged in order to be captured by the Bulldog; in these safety-conscious days, this is the variant now recommended by the Scout Association, among others.

People rarely remember the bruises. But girls often recall that British Bulldog could be especially humiliating, as their knickers were frequently displayed to all and sundry during the mêlée of a capture. Savvier girls of a sensitive age managed to avoid this by wearing shorts under their skirts.

Although some might recognize the game by other names, including 'Across the Middle', 'Cannonball', 'Stampede' and 'Fox and Hounds', it is as British Bulldog that it is most often known, even abroad, though there is a US version known as 'American Eagle'.

British Bulldog can be seen as a sort of elementary version of rugby, that 'thug's game played by gentlemen' as it was once memorably described. Its patriotic title suggests the ultimate playground test of true pluck and grit, of the kind that once built the empire and inspired victory over Nazi Germany. That is, as long as one had a tin of plasters and a cold compress to hand!

PAYING THE PRICE
Forfeits

Lots of games require players to pay a forfeit if they have made an incorrect guess or failed to perform a certain action. Party organizers may find it helpful to have a few ideas up their sleeve, so here are some penalties to dole out:

- Crawl under the table and mew like a cat

- Sing the national anthem (standing up, of course)

- Say 'I met a bull pup up Upper Parliament Street' ten times

- Yawn until you make someone else yawn

- Eat three cream crackers in a minute

- Belly dance for two minutes

- Recite a poem of your choosing

- Recite the months of the year in reverse order

- Put on the socks of the person on your left (having first taken off your own)

- Describe a spiral staircase without using hand gestures

- Peel and eat a banana in ten seconds

- Draw a friend with your eyes closed

- Stick out your tongue and touch your nose with it

- Have lipstick applied to your lips by the person next to you, who must have their eyes closed

- Eat a jam doughnut without licking your lips

- Kiss a pillow as if it is someone you really fancy

- Sit with an ice cube down your shirt

- Make a paper aeroplane one-handed

- Talk about goats (or another random subject) for one minute

- Eat a teaspoonful of Marmite®

The Bumps
Many Happy Returns

Children expect that on their birthday everyone will be nice to them. And, mostly, everyone is. But one tradition would make the typical child dread arriving at school on their birthday: the knowledge that they would immediately be set upon by their friends in order for the Bumps to be bestowed.

The birthday boy or girl would be more or less compelled to lie on the ground, and then a group of friends would grasp them by their arms and legs and 'bump' them up in the air and then down almost to the floor and back up again, once for every year of their life and then once for luck (or sometimes 'one for luck, two for luck and three for the old man's coconut'). If the Bumpee refused to submit peacefully, it was normal for arms and legs to be unceremoniously seized nevertheless, and the child manhandled into the correct position for bumping by a frenzy of eager hands.

What lies behind this bizarre custom? It seems to be intended to attract good luck for the birthday girl or boy on their special day. Though typical of the UK and Ireland, the Bumps are also traditional in other parts of the world, where the idea is to deliver some kind of physical torment to drive away any evil spirits that might be hanging around in the hope of snaffling some birthday cake, or worse.

In Brazil and Italy, the custom is to pull the ear lobes, once for every year of life. In Canada, the birthday boy or girl gets a punch for every year or, in Nova Scotia and Newfoundland, gets their nose greased with butter; apparently, the grease renders the nose too slippery for bad luck to grab someone and pull them away! In Israel and parts of Eastern Europe, the birthday boy or girl sits on a

chair that is then raised and lowered the required number of times.

There is an element of risk in giving or receiving the Bumps, so they should be performed with care, preferably somewhere that the landing is soft. It is a relief to most people when they become too heavy to be given the Bumps on their birthday – one of the few consolations of growing older!

The Buttercup Game

Butter Wouldn't Melt ...

Summer meadows ... bright yellow flowers ... the Buttercup Game. What pastime could be more evocative of the lazy, hazy summer days of our formative years?

The Buttercup Game is so simple to play that it scarcely qualifies as a game at all – more a charmed moment, a childhood initiation into the delights of simple pleasures.

Pick a golden buttercup. The flowers are easy to find, whether growing in garden lawns (to the frustration of keen gardeners), on roadside verges or in fields. Hold the buttercup with the cup side of the flower under the chin of a friend. If it casts a golden glow on their skin, then the friend likes butter, and is told of their taste for it. Repeat with as many friends as are available.

Truth be told, buttercups are so luminously golden that they rarely fail to shine a light. Yet still children hold out their chins, in the solemn belief that the flower will magically reveal their preferences.

It would spoil children's fun to tell them that buttercups are actually rather poisonous little flowers. The plant contains a chemical that can cause inflamation and blistering of the skin on contact and is poisonous if swallowed. Pliny, the Roman historian and botanist, recorded that, when eaten, buttercups 'induced maniacal laughter ending in death'. Luckily, buttercups taste so horrible that would-be buttercup eaters are more likely to spit them out immediately than to swallow them.

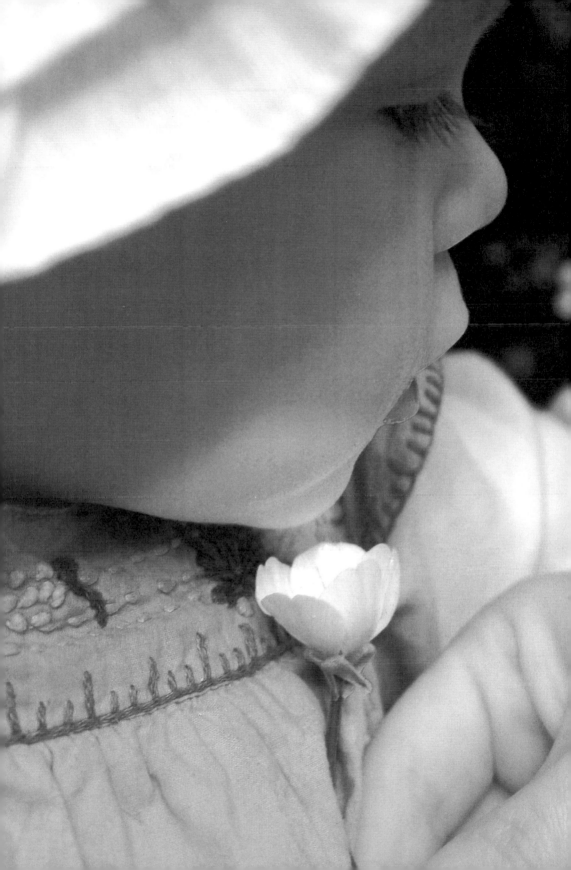

The Buttercup Game

It is said that the tradition of the Buttercup Game comes from medieval times, when people believed that butter made from the milk of cows that ate buttercups was yellower than butter from the milk of those that did not. This might explain the enduring popularity of 'Buttercup' as a name for cows, but, ironically, cows usually avoid buttercups altogether because of their acrid taste!

Happily, no harm is likely to result from picking a flower for a game of Buttercup. It might even herald a romance; according to another folk tradition, the appearance of a yellow glow indicates not that the person has a predilection for a certain dairy product, but that they have a secret admirer. Someone who hopes to butter them up, you might say.

Capture the Flag
Across Enemy Lines

This rumbustious outdoor game is best played by a large group. Two leaders are chosen and each selects a team from the assembled company. Then an area of territory is decided upon, perhaps divided by a natural feature such as a stream or a line of trees, and a 'base' or 'home' for each team is agreed. Finally, each team takes its 'flag' (in practice a coat, handkerchief or other object) and plants it in their home territory in as inaccessible a location as possible.

Each team then tries to capture the flag of the opposition by making sorties, either individually or in groups, into rival territory. Once behind 'enemy lines', however, a player can be taken 'prisoner' by being touched on the shoulder by a member of the opposing team. Prisoners are taken to the rival base, where they must stay until they are rescued by their fellow team members. All prisoners must be rescued before the team is allowed to make a renewed attempt to capture the enemy's flag. The game continues until one team has either captured the flag or had its entire team taken prisoner.

In some versions, prisoners are allowed to make rescue attempts easier by linking hands and standing in a human chain stretching out towards the territory boundary. Other objects can also be substituted for the 'flag', and in some versions of the game numerous different objects must be captured before the game is over. Not surprisingly, Capture the Flag is a game that can go on all day.

The military and territorial resonances of Capture the Flag are even more apparent in some of the jingoistic alternative names for the game. Deriving from traditional rivalries, they include 'French and English', 'Scotch and English', 'Germans and English' and even 'Japs and Russians'.

Capture the Flag was much played in the 18th and 19th centuries, especially in the north of England, but then it seems to have dwindled in popularity. However, it appears to be making a comeback, reinvented for the 21st century as part of the so-called urban gaming trend, where adults play location-based games in city streets, sometimes using mobile phones and other forms of technology to communicate with one another. Such a development only goes to show that the best games are truly timeless.

THE MOTHER OF INVENTION
Children and the Art of Improvisation

In the absence of ready-made toys, necessity and poverty encourage children's innate talent for improvisation. Children in ancient times played with animal bones, stones, sticks and whatever other objects they had to hand, enjoying such timeless games as Marbles and Knucklebones. Conkers has been played not only with horse chestnuts but also snail shells and hazelnuts. And Poohsticks was invented when, in an idle moment, Winnie-the-Pooh dropped a fir cone into a stream.

Sticks are particularly adaptable objects for play, despite the common adult protest 'You'll have someone's eye out with that!'. A stick makes a perfect rifle or six-shooter, a sword or a horse, while a collection of sticks can be used to construct a den.

As well as being essential for a game of Tin Can Tommy, tin cans make excellent and satisfyingly noisy footballs. And who needs a mobile phone? Make a hole in the bottom of two cans (old cocoa tins are particularly good for this) and thread a long piece of string through each hole, knotting it at each end so the cans are joined together. Then pull the string taut and take it

in turns to talk and listen into the cans. Hey presto, a working telephone!

A couple of old bike or pram wheels and a soap box? Why, a bit of tinkering in the shed could produce a go-cart. Can't afford a Barbie? Make a doll from a wooden clothes peg and some scraps of material. Similarly, some string or a few nails can transform two pieces of wood into a perfectly serviceable cricket bat.

With ready-made toys so freely and cheaply available nowadays, such improvisation is rarely forced upon Western youngsters any more. But in impoverished regions, children can still be found improvising toys and games out of tin cans and wire, old inner tubes and bicycle wheels, showing that necessity is still the mother of invention.

Cat and Mouse
The Thrill of the Chase

This traditional chasing game, suitable for six to eight players, is inspired by the traditional enmity between cat and mouse.

One player is chosen to be the Cat, and another to be the Mouse. The remaining players make a ring, holding hands as tightly as they can. The Mouse stands inside the ring, whilst his feline foe prowls round the outside and attempts to break through the circle to catch the Mouse inside. The players in the ring, who are unshakeably on the Mouse's side, must try to stop the Cat from breaking into the ring by closing up tightly to one another.

If the Cat does succeed in slipping through, the Mouse can be released from the ring to assist his escape. If the players are quick, they can lower their arms and catch the Cat in the ring once the Mouse has escaped. If they are too slow, however, and let the Cat out, the Mouse is fair game, although he does have the advantage of being able to slip in and out of the ring unhindered until caught.

In a slightly different version, the players stand in several lines, with four or six players to a line. They hold hands crosswise (as if they were about to sing 'Auld Lang Syne') and face in the same direction. On the word 'Go', the Cat must chase the Mouse up and down and through the lines. When someone shouts 'Turn' or blows a whistle, the players forming the lines turn 90 degrees to the left and grab the hands of the players now standing next to them. This reconfiguration causes confusion for both Cat and Mouse. When 'Turn' is called once more, the players switch back to their original positions. Once caught, the Mouse swaps places with the Cat. After that, two new players are selected for the roles.

The image of a cat and mouse game is frequently called upon to describe the police pursuit of a criminal who is adept at evading arrest. And in his novel *Anna Karenina*, Tolstoy memorably uses the image of the way the game is played to illustrate how Vronsky is still welcome in polite society while his lover, the adulterous Anna, is not.

> *He very quickly perceived that though the world was open for him personally, it was closed for Anna. Just as in the game of cat and mouse, the hands raised for him were dropped to bar the way for Anna.*

So Cat and Mouse is that rare thing: a children's game that has informed a great adult classic of world literature!

Cat's Cradle
String Theory

Cat's Cradle is an intricate string game, particularly popular with girls. It involves the execution of a number of complicated moves by which a loop of string or wool is passed from the hands of one player to the other and back again. There are endless permutations; the most popular are described here. After that, it is all down to the players' ingenuity!

The first player prepares the string, which should be about 120cm long and tied in a loop. Holding her hands up in the air, palms facing, the first player wraps the string around both hands, and then loops both hands under again, so that a second loop of string runs across the inside of each palm. Then she puts the index finger of each hand through the second loop on the opposite hand and pulls the string back across. This is the Cradle (1).

Now the game begins. The second player uses the thumb and index finger of each hand to grasp the cross of string on each side of the Cradle (2), and then pulls these crosses taut and to the sides. Then she takes the strings down and

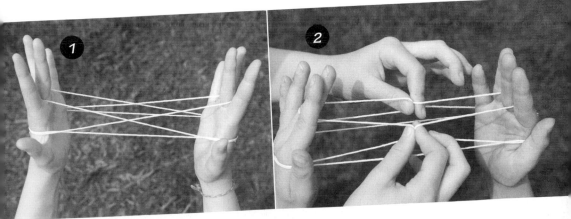

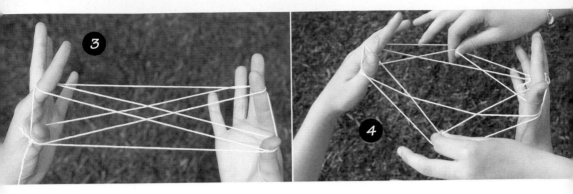

under the Cradle, bringing them up through the middle. As her hands come up through the middle, the first player lets go and the second player simultaneously transfers all the strings to her own hands and stretches them wide. If done correctly, a flat pattern with crossed strings will appear. This pattern is sometimes known as the Soldier's Bed, or the Church Window (3).

The next sequence is performed in similar fashion, by grasping the strings at the crosses, pulling them out to the sides (4) and taking them underneath the Cradle (5). At the end of this second move, a flat pattern of parallel lines known as Tramlines or Candles will result (6). This is tackled using the little fingers. The little finger of the right hand is hooked under the top left-hand string on the outside and this is pulled to the right beyond the outside of the Cradle. Then the little finger of the left hand is hooked under the top right-hand string on the outside and this is pulled to the left beyond the outside of the Cradle (7).

Holding tight to the strings, the player turns her hands and takes them underneath the Cradle (8) and then moves her thumbs and index fingers upwards. The resulting pattern is called the Manger, an upside-down version of the Cradle (9).

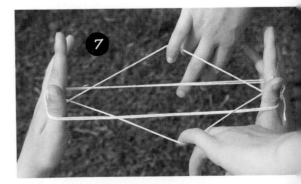

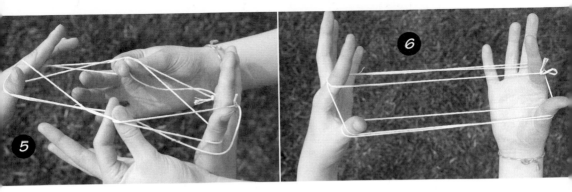

There are numerous permutations on these moves, and the sequence of figures can be altered by tackling the patterns either from above or from below. As long as no-one fluffs a move, the game can go on indefinitely, with players experimenting with the order and direction of moves.

The origins of Cat's Cradle are obscure but probably date back thousands of years. String figures similar to Cat's Cradle are found all over the world and have often been the subject of study by anthropologists investigating the culture of indigenous peoples. Some of these string games can be enjoyed by a person on their own, including a delightful Japanese pastime called *ayatori*. The shapes that can be made in *ayatori* include a broom, an aeroplane, a diamond, a turtle and a Tokyo tower. It is truly remarkable how far one simple loop of string can go – the phrase 'how long is a piece of string' has never seemed so apt.

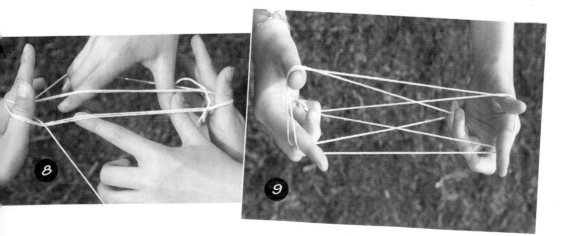

AMUSEMENTS OF THE ANCIENTS
Games in Antiquity

Tomb paintings show that children in ancient Egypt were just as rumbustious as their counterparts today, revelling in racing games, wrestling and tugs of war. They played games with balls made from papyrus and leather, and also at Marbles and Skittles. A scene in a tomb at Beni Hassan in Middle Egypt dating from 2000 BC is believed to show a 'finger-flashing' game similar to Stone, Paper, Scissors. There was even an Egyptian version of Leapfrog, known as khuzza lawizza, in which two children sat on the ground with their hands touching, while another child tried to jump over their arms.

In ancient Greece, children played Blind Man's Buff, as if acting out the part of Polyphemus, the one-eyed Cyclops who was blinded by Odysseus. They played Stone Skimming with oyster shells, a version of Hide and Seek and a kind of Tag. The game of Knucklebones is mentioned both in Homer's Iliad and the Odyssey,

and was a diversion enjoyed by adults as well as children.

Ancient Roman children would also get down and dusty on the ground for a bout of Knucklebones, and may well have followed it up with a game like Noughts and Crosses. Remains of similar playing grids to the ones used on paper today have been found etched into surfaces all over the ancient Roman empire, and some think that *terni lapilli* was an early version of the game. According to one theory, Hopscotch derives from children imitating a Roman training exercise used to improve the footwork of soldiers. An energetic game similar to Husky Bum, known as How Many Horns has the Buck?, would also have been familiar to youngsters in Roman times.

One game known to both the Greeks and the Romans was Morra, a hand game played by two players either for fun, to decide who should go first, or to settle disputes, rather like tossing a coin today. There are many different versions but in one of the most popular, one player was designated 'odd' and the other 'even'. On a signal or count of three, both players brought out a hand from behind their back to show a number of fingers, from none to five. Who won depended on whether the total number of fingers shown was odd or even. Morra is still played today throughout the Mediterranean region.

Not surprisingly, it is difficult to find archaeological evidence for less organized games, but easy to imagine children in the ancient world chasing each other, playing Tag, hiding and seeking, and enjoying all the spontaneous games that come so naturally to children of any era. As Iona and Peter Opie put it: 'If a present-day schoolchild was wafted back to any previous century he would probably find himself more at home with the games being played than with any other social custom.'

Charades
Give Us a Clue

Charades is an activity guaranteed to bring out in its participants any latent talent for pantomime. Since its invention in 16th-century France, where a charade meant any sort of conundrum involving words, the game has been widely played in many different versions, and is a particular favourite at Christmas.

In older versions of Charades, two teams took it in turns to guess at a polysyllabic word that was acted out before them. So if 'butterfly' was the word, the performing team would mime first the word 'butter', then 'fly' and finally 'butterfly'.

This traditional version has been eclipsed in popularity by a newer one derived from a variety of television game shows, most notably *Give Us a Clue*, which aired from 1979 until the 1990s. The more modern version also involves two teams, but instead of performing a word, phrase or proverb, players act out the title of a book, film, television programme, play or song. The list of titles to be acted out can be compiled in advance by each team, the only proviso being that anything too obscure or that only one person has heard of must be excluded. The titles are written on slips of paper and placed in two hats, one in front of each team.

To start, a player from Team A takes a slip of paper from the hat of Team B. He must act out the title for his teammates to guess. A stopwatch can be used to time the proceedings, with each team being given about three minutes to guess as many titles as they can before the other team has its turn.

'Film'

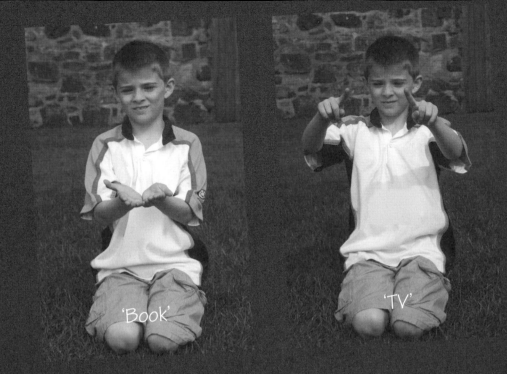

'Book'

'TV'

First, the player performing the mime indicates the category the title falls into, using the following gestures:

Film – mime cranking an old-fashioned cine camera with one hand and hold the other hand up to one eye for the lens.

Book – mime opening a book.

TV programme – draw a square in the air for the screen.

Play – mime pulling a rope to open a theatre curtain, or some curtains being drawn.

Song – mime singing.

Next, the player indicate the number of words in the title by holding up the appropriate number of fingers.

Then, the player indicates which word they are going to mime – one finger means it is the first word, and so on. Players can mime the words in any order; if the fourth word, for instance, is the easiest to mime or will give a strong clue to the whole title, it is a good idea to start with that.

'Fourth Word'   'Third Syllable'

Players can also indicate how many syllables the word has by placing the appropriate number of fingers on one arm, and then indicating which syllable is going to be mimed.

To indicate that they plan to act out the whole title at once, players sweep their arms round in a big circle in the air. Players can also suggest whether the word is short or long using the same method a fisherman would employ to show the size of his catch. Showing that the word is short usually indicates that it is a word like 'the', 'or', 'at' or 'and'. Another useful gesture is to cup a hand behind one ear, which means that the word 'sounds like'.

So if someone had to act out the film title *The King and I*, they would mime that it is a film title (mime that movie camera) of four words (four fingers). If they decided to mime the second word (two fingers) of one syllable (one finger on the arm), they would mime wearing a crown and/or sitting on a throne wearing long robes. They could also mime 'sounds like' and point to a ring. For the fourth word the player could point to himself, and hold up one finger, hoping that eventually someone will realize this means 'I'. By this point, someone should have twigged that the required title is that of a musical set in Thailand and starring Yul Brynner and Deborah Kerr.

Chinese Whispers

Pssst, Pass It On ...

Chinese Whispers is one of those perennially popular party games with which most people are so familiar that they can barely remember the first time they played it. Marvellously simple, it requires neither props nor equipment. A group of four or more people, with their ears pricked, is all that is necessary.

The participants sit in a circle or a line. One person decides on a word or phrase and whispers it into the ear of the person next to them. The recipient then repeats the word or phrase into the ear of the next person, and so on, until the last player has heard the phrase in question. The final player repeats out loud what has been whispered to them. Sometimes the word or phrase will be correct or almost correct, but often it will have become distorted beyond recognition, prompting much hilarity when the original phrase is revealed.

While the phrase in question can become corrupted in the natural process of being whispered from player to player, the practice of deliberately mishearing and mis-repeating the phrase is widespread and usually acceptable. Some players, particularly young children, are apt to forget what has just been whispered to them in any case. All these mishaps only make for a more entertaining game. One classic Chinese Whispers phrase is 'Send reinforcements, we're going to advance', which famously became scrambled into 'Send three-and-fourpence, we're going to a dance.' Tongue twisters are also favourites as they are so easily misheard.

The origin of the name Chinese Whispers is unclear but probably derives from the once prevailing western view of China as a confusing and impenetrable place with numerous languages, all of them apparently

incomprehensible. However, some think Chinese Whispers refers, in a politically incorrect way, to problems that the Chinese were formerly supposed to have in communicating clearly with one another. It is closely related to the term 'Chinese fire drill' used to describe the incompetence of a group in carrying out instructions. This expression, still used in the USA, supposedly derives from a naval incident in the early 1900s involving a British ship crewed by Chinese who misunderstood the procedure for carrying out a fire drill with chaotic consequences.

Any discomfort about calling the game Chinese Whispers can be overcome by using one of its alternative names, which include 'Telephone' (the name by which the game is most commonly known in the USA), 'Family Meals' and 'Secrets'. However, in France the game is called *téléphone arabe*, or 'Arab Telephone', which implies a completely different set of national stereotypes.

Despite its controversial name, Chinese Whispers remains a game worth playing both for its entertainment value and for its educational worth. What better way of teaching children the value of speaking clearly? Or, as exemplified beautifully by Hans Christian Andersen's story about Chinese Whispers, 'It's Quite True!', showing them the dangers of eavesdropping and then repeating something you might not have heard correctly?

Cigarette-card Skimming

Because You're Too Young to Smoke

During the early part of the 20th century, before the dangers became known, almost every adult smoked cigarettes. This near-universal habit provided the younger generation with a plentiful supply of cigarette cards. These small mines of information were to be found inside cigarette packets from the later years of the 19th century, but they appeared in increasing numbers in the decades prior to World War II. After the war, cards were given away with packets of tea instead, heralding the more health-conscious era which was to follow.

During the war years in particular, 'fag cards' were eagerly collected by children in an attempt to make up sets of footballers, flowers, cars, planes or whatever the subject of the moment was; the cards usually appeared in sets of 50. However, because no cards were produced during the war years, the only way to increase one's collection and acquire coveted sets

was either to swap with other collectors or to win cards through one's well-honed skimming skills.

Card-skimming games were played mainly by boys. They were a particularly popular playground pursuit, although many a walk home from school was prolonged by children pausing to skim cards along the way.

There are a number of different card-skimming games, all similar in principle. In one version, a player's card is propped up against a wall or fence. The other players take it in turns to flick their own cards at it, with the aim of knocking it down. A throwing line can be drawn, like the oche in darts. Whoever succeeds in dislodging the propped-up card wins all the cards that have been thrown. If no one succeeds in hitting the target, the player who owns the propped-up card wins all those lying on the ground around it.

In a simpler version, a card is placed on the ground and the other players try to skim their own cards so that one of them overlaps it. Whoever succeeds in doing this first wins all the cards lying on the ground. The simplest version of all involves players competing to see who can skim a card the furthest. The winning player picks up all the cards.

A particularly sophisticated version involves drawing squares on the ground, with a different number in each square, rather like a hopscotch grid. Then the players take it in turn to skim their cards so that they land in one of the squares. The number written in the square where the card lands determines how many cards a player wins. If a player fails to land the card in any square, however, they lose their card.

Skimming or flicking techniques vary. The card can be placed on the left hand, and then flicked away with the middle finger of the right. Or it can be held between the first two fingers of the skimming hand (either left or right depending on the player) and then launched with a rotating motion. Technique is all, unless a sharp cross-wind is blowing or stray dogs get in the way. And it pays to look after the cards, as the more dog-eared the cards become, the less aerodynamic they are.

Nowadays there would be a national outcry if cigarette manufacturers tried to give away with every packet a colourful little collectable attractive to children. Cigarette-card skimming games are a reminder of an innocent age when adults smoked without expectation of repercussions, and eager boy collectors sharpened both their general knowledge and their aim.

Clapping Games
Hand to Hand Co-ordination

Clapping games are as old as the hills – a painting of girls playing a clapping game has even been found on an ancient Egyptian tomb. Playgrounds today still resound to the slap of palm against palm and the chanting of rhymes. As long as there have been children, it seems, they have felt the urge to clap their hands together and sing.

Games require a minimum of two players, who stand facing one another, and close enough to clap their hands against their partner's without having to straighten their arms. There are many sequences of hand movements, but most commonly the rhyme starts with players clapping their own hands together on the first word. On the next word of the song, both hands are clapped, palms outwards, against those of the partner. Next the players clap their own hands together again. Then each player claps their right hand against the right hand of their partner, and on the next word claps their own hands together again. This is followed by clapping their left hands together, and so on. On the final word or words of each verse, both hands are clapped against those of the partner.

Other sequences might involve double claps, clapping high in the air and then low down, clapping vertically with upturned/downturned palms, clapping hands to shoulders or thighs, or holding one hand together with the partner's and clapping the other hands above and below them. The tempo can quicken or slow at any time; the important thing is to stay in time with each other.

Mostly played by girls, clapping games are accompanied by a vast repertoire of songs and rhymes. Some are well-known

and almost universal; some are unique to a particular playground. One of the best-known is the nursery rhyme 'Pat-a-Cake', also the name by which clapping games are sometimes generically known:

> *Pat-a-cake, pat-a-cake, baker's man.*
> *Bake me a cake as fast as you can.*
> *Pat it and roll it and mark it with 'B'*
> *And put it in the oven for Baby and me.*

'B' and 'Baby' are often substituted by participants' own names.

Fascinating regional variants on the same basic rhyme often occur as individual inventiveness comes into play. And some rhymes, such as those mentioning famous people or events, change over time as children substitute contemporary names for those of a previous generation.

But for children the important thing about clapping games is the scope for creativity; the rhymes can be made up and changed at any time by the players, making the games and rhymes an endlessly evolving art form.

Here is just a small selection of some of the most popular rhymes, past and present:

My boyfriend gave me an apple.
My boyfriend gave me a pear.
My boyfriend gave me a kiss on the lips.
And threw me down the stairs.
I gave him back his apple.
I gave him back his pear.
I gave him back his kiss on the lips.
And threw him down the stairs.

My mother said
That I never should
Play with the gypsies in the wood.
If I did
She would say
Naughty girl to disobey.

When Suzie was a baby, a baby Suzie was,
And she went: 'Waa, waa, waa, waa, waa!'

When Suzie was a toddler, a toddler Suzie
*   was,*
And she went scribble, scribble, scribble,
*   scribble, scribble.*

When Suzie was a schoolgirl, a schoolgirl
*   Suzie was,*

And she went: 'Miss, Miss, I can't do
this, I've got my knickers in a right
old mess.'

When Suzie was a teenager, a
teenager Suzie was,
And she went: 'Ooh, ah, I lost my
bra, I left my knickers in my
boyfriend's car!'

When Suzie was a mother, a mother
Suzie was,
And she went: 'Help, help, the baby's
sick! Help, help, the baby's sick!'

When Suzie was a granny, a
granny Suzie was,
And she went knit, knit, 'I dropped
a stitch!'

When Suzie was a skeleton, a
skeleton Suzie was,
And she went rattle, rattle, rattle,
rattle, rattle.

A sailor went to sea, sea, sea
To see what he could see, see, see
But all that he could see, see, see
Was the bottom of the deep blue sea, sea, sea.

My name is
High-Low Jack-alo
Jack-alo High-Low
High-Low Jack-alo
Jack-alo High-Low.

Conkers
I Aimed, I Swung, I Conquered

Each October, the gleaming mahogany nuts of the horse chestnut tree ripen and burst from their prickly casings to land on the ground, where they wait to be claimed by the young, and the young at heart.

Yes, it is conker time, when children everywhere hunt eagerly through the heaps of fallen horse chestnut leaves, or throw sticks up into the branches in the hope of bringing down a real beauty. Prime candidates are pierced with a skewer or other sharp tool and strung on bootlaces, or pieces of string of a similar length, and then – let the conker contests begin!

Conkers

Conkers is believed to have evolved from a game called 'Conquerors' that was originally played with snail shells or, in some later variants, with hazelnuts. But with the spread of the horse chestnut tree throughout Britain following its introduction in the 17th century, its nuts came to predominate and the earlier games were gradually replaced by the version we now know.

There are many regional variations in the rules, and even in the name; it is known in the English Midlands as 'Oblionker' and play is accompanied by chants such as 'Obli, obli, onker, my nut will conquer'. Other childhood lore may dictate that, for good luck, one must proclaim 'Oddly, oddly, onker – my first conker!' upon finding the first conker of the season.

In general, a conker fight involves two players, each with one conker. One player holds out their conker by its string at arm's length from his or her body, while the other player tries to hit it with their conker. Players take it in turns to attempt a hit, and ultimately to smash their opponent's conker. If a player misses, they are permitted up to two more tries. If the strings tangle, the first person to shout 'strings' gets the next shot. The game ends when one conker

breaks. The winning conker is then rechristened according to the number of conkers it has vanquished; if six, then it is a six-er, if nine, it becomes a nine-er.

However, in a more complicated system of scoring, if the beaten conker has previously conquered a number of opponents, the victorious conker adds those to its score. So if a six-er beats a conker that has previously vanquished five opponents (and thus was a five-er), this tough nut would become a twelve-er, made up of its own six wins, plus its latest victim, plus its latest victim's five previous wins.

Not surprisingly, given these somewhat ruthless rules, the game is a competitive business. Though officially frowned upon, there are various recommended techniques for hardening up conkers and making them less susceptible to damage. Some swear by soaking their conkers in vinegar, others by baking them in the oven. A simpler method, though one involving a degree of forward planning, is to put the conkers away in a dark place for a year. They can be retrieved the following season, somewhat duller but rock hard.

Such devious techniques are firmly outlawed at the annual World Conker Championships, which take place on the village green at Ashton in Northamptonshire on the second Sunday in October every year. Here the conkers are provided ready-strung by the organizers for competitors of all ages and nationalities to battle it out. The competition's popularity, like that of the game, shows little sign of abating despite health and safety concerns that have led to it being banned in some school playgrounds in recent years.

Consequences
Paper Folding with a Difference

Consequences is the perfect game for a wet afternoon. It can be played by any number of players but the ideal number is between four and eight. Even young children can join in, as long as they can write simple sentences and come up with wacky ideas.

Each player is given a sheet of paper and a pen or pencil. At the top of page everyone writes down a man's name or the name of a famous man, real or fictional. Then they fold down the paper enough to conceal what they have written, and pass the paper to the player on their left. Next, everyone writes down the name of a female character, and repeats the process of folding and passing on the paper.

In the subsequent rounds players write down:

- The name of a place (real or imagined) where the two people could meet

- What he said to her

- What she said to him

- What the consequence was

- What the world said (ie the moral of the tale)

After the last round, the papers are passed round once more or mixed up in the middle of the table. Then each player unfolds one paper and reads out the story that has been created. The results are always surreal and often highly amusing.

An example could be:

Father Christmas

met

Florence Nightingale

in

A lift.

He said to her,

Do you want chips with that?

She said to him,

My, how you've grown.

The consequence was

They all went home for tea.

The world said

Better late than never.

The game becomes even funnier if, by sheer chance, the story makes sense at some point. But rather than trying to rig the story, the best way to play is by being as random as possible – if players always take their characters from one source, for example *Star Wars* or *Harry Potter*, the game can start to become predictable. The more off-the-wall the suggestions, the better!

A more complicated version has two additional rounds, in which players give adjectives to describe the two characters. So for this version, the first round becomes writing down

Consequences

an adjective or phrase to describe a man, for example 'The incredibly handsome ...'. The third round becomes writing down an adjective or phrase that could describe a woman, for example 'The incredibly gorgeous ...'.

A picture version of Consequences requires players to draw a body in stages. In the first round, everyone draws a head, the more outlandish and personalized the better. Then each player folds over the paper far enough to conceal most of the picture but leaving the lower lines exposed so the next player knows where to join on the next bit.

In the following rounds, players draw:

- a body, with arms

- a pair of legs

- a pair of feet

Which parts of the body are drawn at each stage can be adapted to suit the number and drawing abilities of the players. When the drawings are unfolded, some very eccentric characters are revealed.

BRUEGHEL'S CHILDREN
Games in Early Modern Times

The Flemish painter Pieter Brueghel the Elder (c.1520–69) was particularly fond of painting scenes with lots of figures crowded into a small space. In 1560, he completed the picture known as *Children's Games* in which he captured children engaged in all the popular games and rough-and-tumble activities of the time. The painting packs in over 200 children, mostly in small groups, and but for the clothes the scene has all the characteristics and wild energy of a modern playground. It is remarkable just how many of the activities depicted not only survive but would be recognized by children today. They include:

- Blind Man's Buff
- Bowling
- Follow My Leader
- Hoops
- Husky Bum
- King of the Castle
- Knucklebones (similar to Jacks and Five Stones)
- Leapfrog
- Marbles (two groups of children playing different types)
- Ninepins (or Skittles)
- Tag
- Tug of War
- Wrestling

A few games, however, would be less familiar to today's girls and boys. For instance, Who Will Be My True Love is a rather mysterious diversion in which the players huddle together on the ground. Another player places a coat or blanket on top of them and recites the words 'Who will be my true love?' and then whips the cover off again. Presumably whatever happens under the blanket goes some way towards identifying one's sweetheart.

Or there is Walk the Kettle, a game for two players in which an old kettle or pot is used as a target. One player defends the kettle, moving it around on the ground. The second player tries to hit the moving target with a long stick. The player with the kettle tries to stop this happening while simultaneously trying to avoid being hit with the stick. If the player with the stick strikes and misses, the two players change places.

And then there is Bounce the Sack or More Sacks to the Mill, in which players throw one poor

playmate to the ground, and then fling themselves on top of him with shouts of 'Bags to the mill!': an early precursor of the rugby scrum, perhaps? This game was also known to Shakespeare, who mentions it in *Love's Labours Lost*, first performed c.1594.

Brueghel's painting is now in the collection of the Kunsthistorisches Museum in Vienna.

Cops and Robbers

Bang, Bang, You're Dead!

Make-believe games that pit one adversary or side against another have always been a feature in the playground or street, often despite the best efforts of those who want to encourage non-combative activities.

Among numerous permutations of the conflict game, Cops and Robbers is probably the standard. The scenario of the battle between law-enforcers and criminals is unlikely to fade from the imaginations of children while it is a perennial feature of society at large and the basis of so many television programmes and books.

There are no set rules in Cops and Robbers. In one classic version, there is a bank and a jail. The Robbers rob the bank (stones can be used for gold bars, pieces of paper for banknotes) and make their getaway. The Cops arrive and give chase, usually with much pretend shooting of guns (sticks are an excellent stand-in for toy guns). Robbers who

are caught by the Cops are thrown into jail. The game may involve the tying-up and interrogation of those in custody – no Geneva Conventions here – or the Robbers may get away scot-free. In some cases, an almighty scrap or similar trial of strength takes place to decide which side wins.

'Cowboys and Indians' was once a favourite alternative; indeed, in the heyday of John Wayne and even into the 1960s and 1970s, this version often prevailed over Cops and Robbers. Perhaps this was because of the westerns that peppered the weekend television schedules, and the widespread availability of cap guns. Nowadays, Cowboys and Indians is viewed as politically incorrect, although a version where the Indians break out of the reservations and reclaim their ancestral lands from the Cowboys might be acceptable.

For those growing up during World War II, when the world had seemingly embarked upon a global version of Cops and Robbers, such games took on a particular resonance. Variants featuring opposing armies, such as 'Germans and English', 'Commandoes and Japs' and even 'Greeks and Romans', were widely played throughout the war years and for decades after.

Unsurprisingly, such games are most popular with boys. Girls are often known to join in with the boys' games – at the risk of finding themselves relegated to passive roles, such as Squaw – but in many cases they have evolved their own struggles. In 'Fairies and Witches', for example, it is the Witches who chase the Fairies, rather as the Cops chase the Robbers. If caught, Fairies are sometimes dragged off to the Witches' lair, where they can be stewed and eaten.

Some might characterize these playground struggles between Cops and Robbers, Cowboys and Indians, Fairies and Witches and so on as representing the fight between good and evil. But in practice, there is no moral high ground. Whether a Cop or a Fairy, the aim is victory. The point is to engage fervently with the cause.

Dips
You're It!

ho is going to be 'It'? Such is the quandary that occurs at the beginning of many playground and party games. The solution? Dips.

Dips provide an amusing and mostly fair way for the players of a game to select the first person to take the role of It, On or Catcher. Everyone lines up or stands in a circle, and one person goes round reciting a dipping rhyme. As they say each word, they point at a different player in turn, including themselves. Sometimes the person who is being pointed at as the rhyme ends becomes It. But usually a lengthier process of selection takes place, whereby players are eliminated from the contest one by one until only one person is left and that player becomes It.

There are hundreds of dipping rhymes, many unique to a particular region. They are, almost by definition, nonsensical, but therein lies much of their charm. The following are among the best-known:

Eeny, meeny, miney, mo,
Catch a robber by his toe,
If he squeals, let him go,
Eeny, meenie, miney, mo.

Eeny, meeny, miney, mo,
Put the baby on the po,
When it's done, wipe its
*   bum,*
Eeny, meeny, miney, mo.

One, two, sky blue,
All out, but you.

Ibble, obble, chocolate
*   bobble,*
Ibble, obble, out.

Ip, dip, sky blue,
Who's It? Not you.

Each peach, pear, plum,
Out goes Tom Thumb;
Tom Thumb won't do,
Out goes Betty Blue;
Betty Blue won't go.
So out goes you.

Dips

Dip, dip, dip,
My blue ship,
Sailing on the water
Like a cup and saucer.
Dip, dip, dip,
You are not it.

Ink, pink, pen and ink
Who made that dirty
stink?
My mother said it was
   you.

Two, four, six, eight,
Mary's at the cottage gate,
Eating cherries off a plate
Two, four, six, eight.

Paddy on the railway
Picking up stones;
Along came an engine
And broke Paddy's bones.
Oh, said Paddy,
That's not fair.
Pooh, said the engine driver,
I don't care.

For the 'potato' dip, everyone holds both their fists in front of them. One person goes round using their own fist to touch the top of each held-out fist in turn. The fist that is being hit as they say the word 'more' is out, and must be held behind the back:

One potato, two potato,
Three potato, four,
Five potato, six potato,
Seven potato, more.

The last person still to have a fist held in front of them becomes It.

To prolong the suspense even more, all dipping rhymes can be extended with the words 'O-U-T spells out, so out you must go [with a jolly good push]'.

One of the most intriguing of dips is 'Yan, Tan, Tethera', also used as a way of counting out in northern areas of

England, perhaps when choosing teams. The words mean the numbers one to twenty:

> *Yan, tan, tethera, methera, pimp,*
> *Sethera, lethera, hothera, dothera, dick,*
> *Yan-dick, tan-dick, tether-dick, mether-dick, bunfit,*
> *Yaner-bunfit, taner-bunfit, tethera-bunfit, methera-*
>   *bunfit, gigert.*

The origin of these number words, used in various forms throughout the north of England, remains obscure. They are believed to be a relic of an ancient language, possibly Celtic, that has survived into modern times among northern shepherds for counting their sheep. Not surprisingly, children in these areas adopted the words for their games.

The dips quoted here are the more respectable versions, of course. Children tend to clean up their act when grown-ups are about and, in a reversal of 'not in front of the children', rarely divulge to adults' sensitive ears rhymes such as:

> *Ip, dip, dogshit,*
> *You are not It!*

GAMES FROM THE DARK AGES
Politically Incorrect Pursuits

While it is heartening to realize how many games have survived down the ages, there are a few that have deservedly slipped into obscurity. The names and rules of such pursuits are likely to render even the most enthusiastic of game-players a little squeamish, while guardians of the politically correct will find their hair standing on end at the very thought of such morally suspect activities.

Caveman's Bride

The players are seated in a large ring, each man with his girl partner on his right hand. One man alone has no partner. He is the first Caveman. When the music starts, the Caveman dashes across to any girl in the ring, seizes her wrist and drags her back to be his partner. As soon as they are both seated (not before), the man who is thus left without a companion makes a similar raid and so secures a new Bride. This goes on as long as the music continues, but when the music stops, any couple that is not seated is eliminated, until only one couple is left.

Political Candidates

A group of players – perhaps half a dozen – are nominated to be political candidates and sent out of the room; lots could be drawn for this role. The remaining players decide on a subject for each of the candidates to speak about – the more inappropriate the subject, the better.

Recommended examples include:

A bachelor – the care of babies

A plump girl – how to keep thin

A housewife – deep-sea diving

A clergyman – the language of Billingsgate

A schoolboy – the preparation of sermons

A student – spring-cleaning

Candidates are recalled to the room one at a time and must make an off-the-cuff speech on the subject they are given. After all the speeches have been heard, the other players vote for the candidate they think should win by writing their name on a slip of paper. The candidate with the most votes is elected.

Baste the Bear

Lots are drawn to chose the first Bear, who takes his seat on a stone, holding in his hand one end of a rope about three yards long; the other end is held by the Bear's Master. The rest of the players attack the Bear with twisted handkerchiefs, and the Master endeavours to touch one of them; if he can do so without letting go of the rope or pulling the Bear from his seat, the player that is touched takes the place of the Bear. Each Bear has the privilege of choosing his own Master; being Bear once, or more often, does not excuse a player, if fairly touched, from becoming so again.

Cigarettes

All the players stand on the pavement, except one, who stands in the middle of the road. The players on the pavement pick the brand name of a cigarette (eg Black Cat, Camel, Churchman, Dunhill or Kensitas) and tell each other which they have chosen while keeping the name a secret from the player in the road. Then the person in the road calls out the name of all the cigarette brands they can think of, and if they guess one correctly, the players on the pavement must attempt to run across the road without being tagged.

Slave Market

The most attractive girls present are put up for auction – they may stand on a table if they promise not to giggle, otherwise they stand at one end of the room. Each player is provided with 25 or 60 counters with which he bids for the ladies. The Auctioneer tries to get as good a price as possible, and the players egg one another on to buy while trying to retain as many counters as possible themselves. The winner is the Buyer who has the most Slaves at the end (or if two have an equal number, whoever has the most counters left). There should also be a prize for the Slave who fetched the highest price, and consolation prizes for the Slaves who did not.

Dusty Bluebells
A Shady Pursuit

Ah, the bluebell. The lovely late-spring flower that conjures up a picture of British beechwoods carpeted in blue. And of children playing a very traditional game, dancing round and singing.

In the game, one player is chosen to be It. The rest stand in a circle with a space between each person and their neighbours, and then they all clasp hands and raise their arms to form arches. The player who is It skips in and out of the arches in a movement known as 'threading the needle', and sings the following (to a tune similar to that of 'Bobby Shaftoe'):

> *In and out of the dusty bluebells,*
> *In and out of the dusty bluebells,*
> *In and out of the dusty bluebells,*
> *Who will be my master?*

When the singing stops, the player who is It stops behind the nearest player in the circle and pats them on the shoulder as all the other children sing:

> *Tippy tippy tappy on your shoulder,*
> *Tippy tippy tappy on your shoulder,*
> *Tippy tippy tappy on your shoulder,*
> *You will be my master*

The player who has been patted then becomes It, while the first player grasps their waist and follows behind them in and out of the arches as the Dusty Bluebells verse is sung again. Then the patting process is repeated until most of the players are in a long and chaotic conga line and the circle becomes too small to negotiate.

Dusty Bluebells is also known as 'Dusky Bluebells', 'Shady Bluebells' and even 'Scottish Bluebells'. The game probably derives from an ancient dance included in springtime celebrations and it also has weaving and sewing connotations. Maypole dancing feels like a more sophisticated version of it.

Whatever its origins, Dusty Bluebells remains very popular with young children. And its springtime connotations make it a pleasantly evocative game to play at any time of the year.

The Farmer's in His Den

It's a Dog's Life

The Farmer's in His Den is a very popular game, especially among younger children. To begin the game, a player is chosen to be the Farmer and stands in the middle of a circle formed by the rest of the players. Those in the circle hold hands and sing the following rhyme while dancing around the Farmer:

> *The Farmer's in his den,*
> *The Farmer's in his den,*
> *E-I-E-I, the Farmer's in his den.*

Then, the Farmer must choose a wife. Everyone sings:

> *The Farmer wants a wife,*
> *The Farmer wants a wife,*
> *E-I-E-I, the Farmer wants a wife.*

The Farmer selects a player in the circle to be the Wife, and she (or he!) joins the Farmer in the centre of the circle. Then other verses are sung and at the end of each verse the latest addition to the circle chooses another player to take each of the following roles:

> *The wife wants a child.*
>
> *The child wants a nurse.*
>
> *The nurse wants a dog.*

Once the child chosen to be the Dog goes into the middle, all the players crowd round and enthusiastically pat the Dog – often rather hard – while singing:

> *We all pat the Dog,*
> *We all pat the Dog,*
> *E-I-E-I, we all pat the Dog.*

When the poor Dog eventually emerges from the fray, that player becomes the Farmer for the next round.

To make the game a bit longer, an extra verse can be added:

The Dog wants a Bone.

In this version, it is the Bone that must suffer the vigorous pats of fellow players, to the strains of 'We all pat the Bone'.

There are many variants on the theme, the most notable of which introduce cows, cats, rats and cheese. One such version finishes with the Cheese in the middle of the circle rather than the Dog or Bone, but no patting is involved. Instead everyone sings a last verse that goes 'The Cheese stands alone', while the Cheese (perhaps a particularly pungent variety?) stands sadly in the middle of the circle.

Instead of singing 'E-I-E-I', you can also substitute 'Hi-ho, the cherry-o', or 'E-I, the andi-o', or 'E-I, addy-o' or 'Hi-ho, the derry-o'. The game is also widely known as 'The Farmer's in His Dell', particularly in North America.

Farming might be a dwindling occupation in reality, but the appeal of being the farmer in this delightful game will surely continue to attract young children for many years to come.

Follow My Leader
Do As I Do

What could be simpler than the game of Follow My Leader, or 'Follow the Leader' as it is also called? One person is chosen to be the Leader and everyone else has to trail behind them in a line and copy everything they do: hopping on one leg, sticking their tongue out, spinning around and so on. Anyone who fails to copy the actions is out of the game.

To ensure that the game proceeds along democratic, rather than autocratic, lines, a change of leader is instituted every so often. The second in line can take over while the leader goes to the back, and so on, until everyone has had a turn.

In an entertaining variation known as 'Leading the Blind', the followers are all blindfolded and are led up hill and down dale by the Leader, each hanging on to the person in front in a desperate attempt to keep up.

Another version of Follow My Leader is more inclusive since it allows everyone to initiate an action. The first person might nod their head twice. The next person repeats this action, and adds another, for example clapping their hands twice. The third person repeats the first two actions and adds yet another. And so it goes on, until there are so many actions to remember that someone gets it wrong and goes out of the game. Play continues until only one player has not been eliminated.

Follow My Leader can also be turned into a circle game with shades of Wink Murder. One person is chosen to be It and leaves the room. The other players choose a Leader and form a circle. When It comes back into the room, they stand in the centre of the circle. The Leader subtly begins to perform an action, the slower the better, such as scratching their ear. Everyone else copies the Leader and It has to guess who the Leader is.

For older children, Follow My Leader often takes on a more challenging character and starts to resemble games like Truth or Dare. Here the Leader will perform a nerve-racking feat, such as walking along a high wall or riding a bicycle up a steep bank. His followers must do the same or risk being branded cissies or ostracized by the gang. Needless to say, such challenges have often led to accidents.

Follow My Leader appeals to children's general predilection for copying one another, hence the indignant cries of 'Copycat!' that often echo round the playground. Follow My Leader is a charming and safe game as long as the activities are not too dangerous – and as long as your Leader does not answer to the name 'Pied Piper'!

Four Corners
Don't Get Cornered!

Four Corners is an energetic indoor game, popular in schools and with Cub and Brownie packs. The rules are simple, and it is a perfect way to work off children's excess energy.

Number the four corners of the room from one to four, or give each a name. Choose one player to be It. The person who is It stands to one side with their eyes closed, then everyone else chooses a corner to stand in. When everyone has chosen, It calls out the number or name of one of the corners. All the players who chose that corner are out of the game and must sit down. The player who is It closes their eyes again and the remaining players again choose a corner, either a different corner or the same one. Then another name or number is called out, and more players are eliminated.

When four or fewer players are left in the game, each must choose a different corner. If It calls out a corner in which no-one is standing, they must call again. The game continues until only one player is left in. That player becomes It for the next game.

To add a little variety, different designations can be used for each corner, such as colours, or suits from a pack of cards. To make the game more challenging, change the name of each corner after every round using removable coloured stickers. This makes it harder for the person who is It to get players out by listening to their movements.

French Cricket
Howzat?

This is the beach holiday classic, but it is also suitable for any grassy area, whether on holiday or closer to home. All that is needed is a cricket bat or tennis racquet and a ball, plus half a dozen or so willing players, although in practice any number of people can play. Fortunately, French cricket is much simpler than normal cricket, the rules of which baffle many adults, let alone children.

The batsman stands in the centre of the playing area with the bat and everyone else fields. The fielders take it in turn to bowl the ball, usually a tennis ball, underarm at the batsman. The bowler tries to hit the batsman on the leg below the knee. The batsman must fend the ball away from his legs with the bat while also trying to hit the ball.

If the batsman manages to hit the ball, he can score 'runs' by making a full circle of his body with the bat, passing it from hand to hand. When a fielder retrieves the ball, he becomes the bowler and has to bowl from whatever position he finds himself in. The batsman, who is not allowed to move his feet, must twist his body round to play the next ball from a new angle. If he moves his feet or topples over, he is out! The batsman is also out if he is caught by a fielder, or if the bowler succeeds in hitting his legs below the knee. The successful bowler or fielder then becomes batsman. The player who scores the highest number of runs is the winner.

Sometimes, the rule is that the batsman is only allowed to turn to face the next delivery if he actually hits the ball. If he misses it, he must play the next ball without turning towards it.

As far as anyone knows, French Cricket is not actually French. The name seems to have been applied just to distinguish this version from its English counterpart, although some think that the reason is because the usual batting stroke is similar to that used in croquet, a game usually assumed to be French because of its name.

For many, though, the precise rules and origins of French cricket are not particularly important. The game's appeal lies more in the memories it evokes of times spent on the beach or in the park with all the family, playing on and on as the shadows lengthen until finally it is time to go home. The adult players are slightly wayward after a few beers at the lunchtime picnic; the younger players are dead keen to get their parents and relatives out, or to sky a ball way over their heads when batting. French cricket symbolizes summer, the great outdoors and kinship with friends and family.

French Skipping
Cat's Cradle for the Feet

Many a girlhood has included hours of playing French Skipping, or 'Elastics', both in the school playground and at home. The game requires three players; two players (the Enders) stand facing each other, using their legs to stretch a big loop of elastic taut between them, and the third leaps in and out of the loop in a series of elaborate prescribed moves.

The classic basic move is Inside, Outside, Inside, On. To perform it, the player starts with both feet inside the elastic, then jumps to get both feet outside the loop and straddle it, then jumps both feet back inside again, before finally jumping so that each foot is on top of each side of the loop, with the elastic caught on the ground under their feet. Sometimes the player faces sideways for the last move.

There are lots of other variations on these basic moves, and some intriguing rhymes to chant as they are performed.

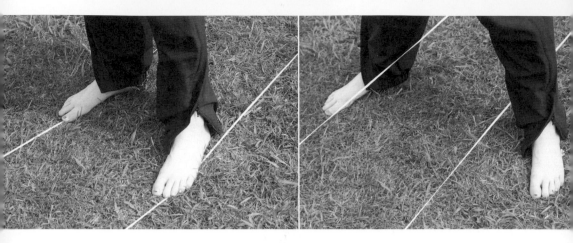

These include:

> England, Ireland, Scotland, Wales, Inside, Outside,
> Inside, On.

> Banana Splits, Banana Splits, Ibble, Obble, Chocolate
> Bobble, Banana Splits.

> Chocolate cake, when you bake,
> How many minutes will you take?
> One, two, three, four.

Perhaps the most memorable are the rhymes that recount episodes from the childhood of Suzie the Schoolgirl (see Clapping Games, p44, for the full version). The part which always induced the naughtiest giggles goes:

> When Suzie was a teenager, a teenager she was.
> And she said 'Ooh, aah, I lost my bra, I left my
> knickers in my boyfriend's car.

All the moves are initially performed with the elastic at ankle height. If this opening round is successfully completed, the elastic is raised to knee height ('kneesies'), then to thigh height ('thighsies') and finally to the waist ('waisties'). If a player makes a false move or falls over, the turn passes to another player.

If Mum's sewing basket failed to yield a sufficient length of elastic (a piece 3m/10ft long was about right), girls would

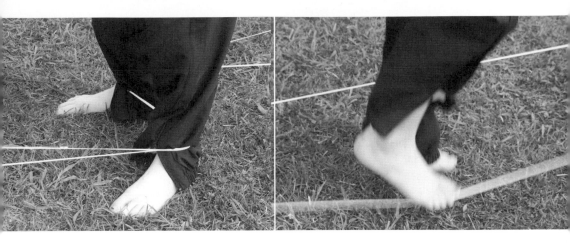

often make do with shorter lengths tied together. Some even looped elastic bands together; perhaps this gave rise to 'Twang', one particularly evocative alternative name for the game.

The white knicker elastic most often used would invariably get grubby and frayed after hours of playing. The footwear often favoured for school in days past, T-bar shoes, were partly responsible for this, as the elastic would get caught round the buckle, sometimes tripping up a player or at least putting them out of the round. But real enthusiasts rarely let such trifles deter them. They would often practise their moves at home, with the elastic stretched between the legs of two chairs.

French skipping is believed to have originated in China or Japan in the 1920s and 1930s, which would explain its alternative names of 'Chinese Skipping' or 'Chinese Ropes'. The game is supposed to have been brought to Britain by US air force families during World War II, and within a couple of decades it had become widely played and wildly popular here.

Recently, French skipping has undergone something of a revival and brightly coloured, purpose-made elastic loops are now available, with painted butterflies to tie them up. The cost of these posh contemporary accessories is much higher than the price once charged by Woollies for a card of knicker elastic. But then, can one still buy knicker elastic nowadays?

Grandmother's Footsteps

We're Behind You

Grandmother's Footsteps is the best-known version of a number of chasing games that have delighted children for generations.

Usually played outside, the game starts with one player being chosen to be the Grandmother. The Grandmother stands by a wall or at the end of a room with their back to the rest of the players, who arrange themselves in a line some distance away or at the other end of the room.

While Grandmother's back is turned, the other players try to sneak up on her without being seen. As soon as Grandmother hears a sound she whips round, and sends any player she sees moving back to the start again. The winner is the player who succeeds in touching Grandmother without being seen. They become the next Grandmother.

A variety of tactics are adopted during a typical game of Grandmother's Footsteps. Some players attempt to sprint up to Granny: a daring but risky tactic. Others cunningly inch their way forwards, a technique that is plodding but less likely to be detected.

In some versions, the Grandmother must spell out a word or say a phrase under her breath before turning round. These include 'L-O-N-D-O-N', 'Crack, crack the biscuit tin' and 'One, two, three, four, five jam tarts'. Sometimes, there is a race back to the finish line once the Grandmother has been touched.

Grandmother's Footsteps also has a variety of quaint regional names, including 'Peep Behind the Curtain',

'Victoria', 'Sly Fox', 'Creepy Jinny', 'Black Pudding' and 'Fairy Footsteps'.

A closely related and equally popular game is 'What's the Time, Mr Wolf?'. Instead of Grandmother, the players creep up on Mr Wolf. The difference is that before each move they make, they must call out 'What's the time, Mr Wolf?'. Mr Wolf says a time, and the other players take that number of paces towards him, calling out each step as they go. So if Mr Wolf declares it is 'Eight o'clock', they can take eight steps.

However, at any point in the game, Mr Wolf might choose to respond 'Dinner time!', at which point he turns and chases all the players back to the start line (it is traditional to scream loudly while being chased). Anyone he catches must take his place as Mr Wolf.

This game is also known as 'What's the Time, Mr Fox?' and 'What's the Time, Mr Bear?', although Mr Wolf is by far the most popular villain.

Hand Shadows

Shine a Light

It is one of the vivid memories of childhood: lying in bed waiting for sleep, which does not come, and feeling a bit scared of things that go bump in the night. A torch will keep the monsters at bay, and sometimes a book might be read under the covers by torchlight; but playing around with the torch one night the realization dawns that all sorts of interesting shadows can be made on the wall.

Shadow games have been entertaining people for centuries, although their popularity has waned since the invention of the electric light bulb made possible a bright, even light throughout any room. But in the days when the flames of candles and oil lamps cast long shadows in the parlour of every home, shadows were an entertainment for young and old alike. Hand shadows were all the rage in Victorian times, when numerous books explained how to make them and even how to put on shadow performances of such popular stories as 'Babes in the Wood'.

Though experts in shadow art can make hundreds of different shadows, beginners find it easier to start with some simple animal shapes:

Dog – place the palms of the hands together, as if clapping the hands. Make a gap between the little fingers and the other fingers. Cross the thumbs and stretch them away from the fingers.

Dove – hold the hands out with the palms facing towards the body. Cross the hands at the wrist, and

cross the thumbs. Stretch the
hands away from the thumbs,
to make a wider angle between
the two. Flap the hands to simulate
flying. The Butterfly is made in the
same way, but the dexterous can pinch a
long thin strip of paper between the thumbs
to make the antennae.

Duck – hold out one hand with the palm facing the floor.
Stretch out the third and little fingers and bring the thumb
up underneath to meet them so that the fingertips touch.
Then crook the first and second fingers up above them to
make an eye.

Crocodile – hold out one hand with the palm facing the
floor. Turn the thumb underneath the fingers. Place a coin
between the first and second fingers so that it pokes out
above them and forms an eye socket.

A trickier shadow is the Swan. Stretch out one arm and
bend the lower arm at the elbow so that it is at right angles
to the upper arm. Bend the hand at the wrist so that it is at
right angles to the lower arm. Stretch out the fingers and
place the thumb underneath, as for the Crocodile. Then
bring the other arm across and rest the other hand on
the upper arm just below the crooked elbow and with the
fingers fanned out. These are the feathers.

Simplest of all is that cute little Bunny. Hold up one hand
and bend down into the palm the thumb and the fourth
and little fingers. Stretch out the other two fingers to form
the bunny ears. What's up, Doc?

Hangman
A Game of Life and Death

Bored waiting for that restaurant meal to arrive? Stuck on a platform waiting for a train that has been delayed? Raining again? Time can be whiled away with a piece of paper, a pencil and some interesting words and phrases in a game of Hangman.

To start, one player thinks of a word or phrase and then writes down a dash to represent each letter, leaving a space between words. Care should be taken to get this right in order to avoid embarrassment later.

The other players take turns to call out a letter of the alphabet. If the letter appears in the word or phrase, the first player writes it in the appropriate gap or gaps. If it does not appear, the player draws one line of the scaffold.

The scaffold generally consists of about five separate straight lines, plus a rope. The condemned man is usually drawn in the following order:

- head
- body
- right arm
- left arm
- right leg
- left leg

Hangman

Once the figure is complete, he is hanged! So in a typical game, players can guess a maximum of twelve letters unsuccessfully before the game is over. To help players remember which letters have already been called out, a list can be kept on the side of the paper.

Play continues until either the word or phrase is correctly guessed and the condemned man is reprieved, or all the lines of the scaffold and condemned man have been drawn, leaving the victim hanging and the word incomplete.

Most players suggest the vowels and other commonly occurring letters in their first guesses; it would be foolish to start by calling out Z, Q or X. However, these tactics can go awry if a word like 'rhythm' or 'quartz' or 'zulu' has been chosen to bamboozle players.

The game of Hangman probably dates back to the 19th century, when public hangings were still a feature of everyday life. The last hangings in Britain took place in 1964, and the days of the death penalty are a dim memory. Now the only time the noose gets tightened is when too many guesses fail in game of Hangman.

The Hat Game

Titfer Tat

The Hat Game, also called Names in the Hat, is an entertaining party game for older children or adults, and one that can get very competitive.

To play, take one hat, lots of slips of paper and a pen for each player. The players form two teams, with the exception of one player who acts as referee. Give each person 10 to 15 slips of paper. All the players write the name of a well-known person, dead or alive, real or fictional, on each of their pieces of paper. The slips of paper are then folded up and placed in the upturned hat.

Choose a team to start, and a player from that team to go first. On the word 'Go' the player draws a name out of the hat, and describes to their team the person whose name is on the paper, but without saying the name or any other words written on the paper. For example, a clue to Robin Hood would be to say 'an outlaw in Sherwood Forest', or for Mary Poppins, 'a famous nanny played by Julie Andrews'.

The Hat Game

As soon as the identity of the person has been guessed correctly, the player draws out another name. This process continues until the time – one to two minutes – is up. The team scores a point for each correctly identified name. Now the teams swap roles, with a player from the other team giving clues to their team. Play alternates between the teams, with each player taking a turn at giving the clues, until all the slips have been drawn from the hat. The team with the highest score wins.

Spelling out the name of the mystery person is regarded as cheating, and such 'clues' lose a point for the team. It is acceptable (but a cop-out) to resort to rhymes, such as 'His first name rhymes with "from", his second with "bones"' (Tom Jones).

It is best to stick to characters known to most of the players, especially when playing with children. The game is less entertaining if names are too obscure for other players to guess.

However, it is possible to give clues to a name even if it is an unfamiliar one. For example, a player might say 'I don't know who this is but his first name is the same as Prince Charles' younger son, and his second name is the word for someone who makes things out of clay' (Harry Potter).

In a saucier version of the game, the players guessing the names can win extra points for the names of known spouses and lovers of the character. So if the answer is Brad Pitt, the team would score extra for 'Angelina Jolie', 'Jennifer Aniston', etc; in this version, though, Casanova might present a challenge!

For a further challenge, after a game, all the names can be put back into the hat and used again but with the clues restricted to three words. A final round might reduce this to one word, hand gestures or even miming.

The Hat Game is also known as 'Celebrity'. In these days of obsession with the lives of the rich and famous, what game could be more deserving of a revival?

Headstands and Handstands, Cartwheels and Crabs

Up and Down and Round We Go

In the summer months, when at last it is possible to play on the grass, informal gymnastic displays can be seen in playgrounds the length and breadth of the country as children show off the latest moves they have perfected. This is particularly so among girls, although boys sometimes hang around to taunt any girl who puts her knickers on show while executing a handstand; some girls try to avoid this humiliation by tucking their skirt into their knicker legs.

Kicking one's heels wildly in the air while trying to perform a handstand is one of the essential experiences of childhood. The most proficient can hold the position high in the air for several seconds unaided. Many others collapse in a heap having scarcely got their legs off the ground. The act is easier to accomplish if the handstand is against a wall; it is common in some school playgrounds to see a whole line of girls with their heads dangling upside down and their feet up an outside wall.

Headstands require a strong triangular base of head and hands. A soft surface is preferable, and a cushion definitely helps. The performer has to settle into position with her head on the ground, hands shoulder width apart, and then quickly whip up her legs to a bent and tucked-in position. At this point she will feel the pressure on the top of her head and start to go a bit red in the face, but if she manages to maintain her balance, she can gradually straighten out

her legs to an almost elegant posture – one beloved of yoga devotees for its ability to strengthen the wrists, arms and shoulders and calm the mind, although these are never considerations in the playground.

The suppler girls are also able to assume the crab position. This involves curving the body over and stretching it upwards while supported on the arms and legs, with the head hanging down backwards. The effect is complete if the performer can move around in a convincing imitation of a crustacean on a beach.

Perhaps the most challenging move of all is the cartwheel. Never has a move looked so effortless in performance, or been so difficult to execute in reality. Long before footballers incorporated cartwheels into their goal celebrations (in those days they just shook hands and got on with the game), girls would spend hours trying to get the spokes of that wheel to revolve in the right order. The trick is to think 'hand, hand, foot, foot' for the sequence in which the limbs touch the ground, and to kick the legs up and over the top rather than out to the side. It is useful to practise on a line to acquire the technique of going straight and to get used to keeping the arms and legs straight; bent legs look terrible. Hours of practice are necessary to get it right, but when you do, oh, the exhilaration!

Here We Go Round the Mulberry Bush

Porridge and Silk

Here we go round the Mulberry Bush,
The Mulberry Bush,
The Mulberry Bush.
Here we go round the Mulberry Bush
On a cold and frosty morning.

This popular action game is performed by walking or skipping round in a circle while singing the song to the same tune as 'Nuts in May'. Everyone stops walking or skipping to mime the various actions described in the verses, which take the following form:

This is the way we wash our face,
Wash our face,
Wash our face.
This is the way we wash our face
On a cold and frosty morning.

Almost any everyday activity can be used as the subject of a verse; for example:

This is the way we brush our teeth ...
This is the way we comb our hair ...
This is the way we sweep the floor ...

The more energetically the actions are performed, the more fun the song will be, particularly for younger children who are becoming coordinated enough to do things for themselves. Hard-pressed parents might want to sneak in some hints, such as 'This is the way we clean our rooms ...', or 'This is the way we stack the dishwasher ...'!

There can be as many variations on the theme as the players want. Traditional variations include the changing of the last line of each verse from 'On a cold and frosty morning' to 'So early in the morning' or 'So early Monday morning' (and then change the next verse to give the next day of the week, etc). Other traditional verses, with their accompanying actions, include:

> *This is the way we go to school*
> [a slow walk]
>
> *This is the way we come from school*
> [a fast walk or skip]
>
> *This is the way the soldier goes*
> [a march]
>
> *This is the way the beggar goes*
> [put hand out]
>
> *This is the way the lady goes*
> [lift an imaginary long dress]

But what is the origin of the Mulberry Bush? Wakefield in Yorkshire claims that the song originated in the city's jail, where prisoners walked round a mulberry bush in the centre of the exercise yard (apparently, the bush thrives there to this day). Certainly mulberry bushes were often planted in prison yards, and the phrase 'been round the mulberry bush' was a euphemism for having spent time in prison.

There is a possibility that the song has even older origins. The mulberry bush is the stuff of legend, associated with

the mythical lovers Pyramus and Thisbe; their fatal clandestine meeting was by a mulberry tree whose white fruit was then stained crimson by their blood. People once danced round mulberry trees on Midsummer's Eve to ward off evil, although that custom does not explain the reference to 'a cold and frosty morning'. The song is most likely to date from the late 17th century, when mulberry bushes were much more common in Britain because of attempts to create a domestic silk-weaving industry.

Despite its intriguing origins, the longevity of Here We Go Round the Mulberry Bush lies in its adaptability, allowing it to be altered to suit the domestic preoccupations of any age. 'This is the way we surf the Net' may arrive in our playgrounds any time now.

Hide and Seek
Coming Ready or Not

Hide and Seek is a simple game, and one that is universal. It requires no special equipment and can be played by any number of players of virtually any age. Hide and Seek (also known as 'Hiding Seek' or 'Hide and Go Seek') lends itself equally to outdoors – assuming that the local landscape can provide the odd bush, tree or shed to hide behind – or to rainy-day fun for those cooped up indoors.

One player is chosen to be the Seeker or It. They close their eyes and count up to an agreed number (normally 100) while the other players run off and hide. Hiding places must usually be found within set boundaries, for example within a garden or in certain rooms of a house. After counting, the Seeker sets off in search of the other players, usually after first calling out 'Coming, ready or not'. Sometimes other rhymes are used instead, such as 'All in, all in, wherever you are, The monkey's in the motor car' in Plymouth, or 'Whether you run or not, I will catch you hot' in Norwich.

In some versions, the Seeker must tap the Hiders on the shoulder to put them out of the game. Usually, the player who is found first becomes Seeker for the next round, while the last player to be discovered is declared the winner. There are versions of the game in which players who have hidden themselves try to slip back to an agreed base without being seen. If they manage to get back undetected they are 'safe'. In an Elizabethan version of the game, the first player to return to the base unseen was known as the 'King', and became 'Seeker' for the next round. An ancient Greek game known as *Apodidraskinda* was also played in this way.

Hide and Seek

Perhaps the most famous variation on Hide and Seek is 'Sardines'. In this, only one person goes off to hide while the rest of the players count to 100. They then disperse to find the lone Hider. If one of them succeeds, they hide with the concealed player until only one person is left seeking while the rest are sandwiched silently together like the proverbial sardines in a tin. This can either be thrilling in its intimacy or something of a torment.

An extra frisson is added to Hide and Seek when it is played after dark. Then it is known by a variety of names, such as 'Cat's Eyes' and 'Ghosts', that conjure up the spookiness of the situation. There are also many regional variations, including 'Chip and Chap' (played up and down trees in Ipswich), and 'Over the Fences' (played between several back gardens in Glasgow).

The possibilities of this game are endless, and no doubt children have been playing versions of Hide and Seek as long as there have been objects to hide behind. Perhaps it was even played in cave and forest in primeval times, when being able to conceal oneself from imminent danger was a skill well worth honing.

Hopscotch
The Eternal Game

One of the most familiar of all playground games, Hopscotch, known in some places as 'Potsie' or 'Pottsie', is also one of the oldest. There are claims that it originated in China, in around 2000 BC, with versions of the game also known to the ancient Egyptians and Greeks. Others believe that Hopscotch was invented by the Romans as a training exercise to improve the footwork of soldiers, who would run the 100ft-long courts in full armour and with heavy backpacks. Roman children imitated the soldiers, drawing out smaller versions of the court and inventing their own rules. And thus Hopscotch spread to countries throughout the Roman Empire, including Britain, and now versions are played all over the world.

The name Hopscotch has nothing to do with Scotland, where it is known as 'Peevers', a 'peever' being the tile or other small object used as the marker. The word Hopscotch comes from 'hop' plus 'scotch', from an Old French word meaning 'to cut' that is also the source of 'scratch' and which describes the scratching out on the ground of the hopscotch court. This ancient means of marking out the court gave way in more recent times to the use of chalk to draw the grid on the pavement or playground. These days, many playgrounds and parks have hopscotch grids painted on the ground. However, care is needed in siting a court in school playgrounds; classroom windows have fallen victim to the great gusto boys can bring to the game because the court was too near the building!

In the classic version of Hopscotch, the court consists of about ten boxes large enough for a player's feet to fit into without overlapping the edges. The boxes are arranged in an alternating pattern of a single box and a pair of boxes drawn side by side, and they are numbered from one upwards. The first player tosses a marker – a small stone, tin lid, bottle cap or coin – into the box numbered one on the court. The marker must land completely within the box, otherwise the turn passes to the next player. If the marker lands correctly, the player hops and jumps through the court to the final square, landing a foot in each box except the one with the marker in it. Players hop into single squares and jump into a pair of squares with a foot in each square. At the end of the court, the player turns and hops through the court in reverse order, picking up the marker on the return journey. Then the player throws the marker into the box numbered two and starts again, and so on. If a player steps on a line, misses a square or falls over, their turn is over and the next player has a go. The first player to complete the course is the winner.

Contemporary versions of the game are a far cry from its rumoured origins in ancient China, where the marker was said to represent the human soul and the game a quest for eternal life. If a player wobbled along the way it was because his soul was weak. So he would work on his hopscotch technique, purifying his soul in the process. Upon successfully reaching 'heaven' at the end of the hopscotch court, having avoided stepping on any lines (so keeping his life free of uncertainty), the player placed the marker representing his soul under his arm or on his head, symbolizing thus the merging of soul and body.

Hot Potato

Can You Handle It?

Hot Potato is a lively game involving suspense, listening skills and considerable hand–eye coordination.

One person is chosen to be the Caller (this could be an attendant adult). The other players sit in a circle and pass round a small object – a soft ball, a bean bag or even a potato. Each player takes the object and passes it on without throwing it. The Caller, who sits with their back to the proceedings, suddenly calls out 'Hot!'. The player holding the hot potato at the time is out. The 'potato' continues to be passed round until only one player is left, and they are declared the winner.

Hot Potato can also be played to music, with a player being eliminated each time the music stops. For extra excitement, a raw egg or a water-filled balloon can be substituted for the potato, although this variation can get messy!

A more energetic version, ideal for outdoor play, has the players standing in a circle and passing or throwing a soft object (such as a beach ball) between them. For this fast and furious variation, players need to be especially quick off the mark if they are to avoid being eliminated. To add extra tension, the Caller can follow the shout of 'Hot Potato' with a countdown from ten. When the countdown ends, the player left holding the ball goes down on one knee, making it much harder to participate. If a player is caught with the Hot Potato a second time, they must go down on both knees. If they are caught out a third time, they are out.

The origins of Hot Potato are obscure. One theory is that it derives from a 17th-century game in which players sat in a row or circle and passed round a lighted taper or candle, while saying 'Jack's alive and likely to live. If he dies in your hand, you've a forfeit to give'. If the flame went out while someone was holding the taper, they were given a forfeit to pay or perform.

Presumably, it is the association with this game that led to the phrase 'hot potato' being used to describe a tense or controversial issue or situation. The phrase is also Cockney rhyming slang for a waiter. Playing Hot Potato at a restaurant table is inadvisable, however, even if spuds are on the menu.

Hunt the Slipper
Seek and Ye Shall Find

Take one slipper – carpet, bedroom or otherwise – and sit all the players in a circle, except for one. The players in the circle are the Cobblers. The other player sits in the middle of the circle and is the Customer. The Customer closes their eyes and says:

> Cobbler, cobbler, mend my shoe.
> Get it done by half-past two.

While this rhyme is recited, the Cobblers pass the slipper round the circle behind their backs. The Customer says:

> Cobbler, cobbler, tell me true,
> Which of you has got my shoe?

On the word 'shoe', the Cobblers stop passing the slipper and the player who is holding it makes sure it is hidden behind their back. The Customer opens their eyes and has to guess who has the slipper by looking at their faces to see who looks guilty. If the Customer guesses wrongly, they must change places with the person who holds the slipper.

The Cobblers can confuse the Customer, and stop any cheating by peeping, if they all keep their hands moving behind their backs whether they are passing the slipper or not.

Hunt the Slipper has long been a popular parlour game, particularly in Victorian times. However, its origins go back to at least the 18th century. Oliver Goldsmith includes a description of the game in his novel *The Vicar of Wakefield*, published in 1766:

> 'the company at this play plant themselves in a ring upon the ground, all except one, whose business it is

HUNT THE SLIPPER.

THE children sit on the ground, or on low seats in a circle, with their knees raised. One has been left out; she brings a slipper, and giving it to one child says:—

"COBBLER, cobbler, mend my shoe,
Get it done by half-past two."

She goes away, and comes back in about a minute and asks if it is done. (During this time the slipper has been passing round.) The

to catch a shoe, which the company shove about under their hams [thighs] from one to another, something like a weaver's shuttle'.

In France, the game is known as *le jeu du fure,* 'the ferret game'. Perhaps the slipper is an inanimate substitute for a furry but slippery animal. If this is the case, then the fluffier the slipper, the better!

Hunt the Slipper is the most widely known of a number of party games that involve guessing the whereabouts of a smallish object. Other versions substitute for the slipper objects such as a thimble, an orange or a ring, which can be passed along a ribbon held behind the backs of all the players.

Hunt the Slipper and its variations are excellent preparation for adult life. For parents, the phrase 'Have you seen my ... ?' is an all too commonly heard refrain. The ability to hunt down a wide variety of objects under time pressure is a valuable talent, as is the capacity to interpret correctly the guilty look on a child's face as to what they have concealed about their person.

Husky Bum

Only the Strong Survive

Husky Bum is a very physical game that was all the rage, particularly in northern England and the Midlands, until the 1950s. It was particularly popular with boys.

Two teams of around six players are organized and the players decide which team will do the jumping first. One player from the other team stands against a wall facing outwards to act as a cushion. The rest of his teammates line up one behind the other, with their heads between the shoulders or legs of the person in front of them, similar to a rugby scrum but in a straight line. The line anchors itself to the player against the wall for support. It is advisable for the team's strongest player to be at the back.

Then, one at a time, the rival team's members run up to the line from behind and leap onto the back of a child as far towards the front of the line as possible. Inevitably, most of the jumping team end up on the backs of the supporting team members at the back of the line. Easing oneself along the line after making one's jump is not allowed, nor is steadying oneself by putting a foot on the ground. Taking flying leaps and making crushing landings in the hope of collapsing the line are, however, permissible. The members of the team underneath are allowed to defend themselves by bouncing and shaking.

If the line does collapse, the jumping team wins and has another go. But if the line holds firm even with all the rival team on top, the leader of the jumping team holds up either a finger or a thumb out of sight and asks 'Husky bum, finger or thumb?'. The leader of the team underneath

Husky Bum

has to guess which is being held up. If they guess correctly they get a chance to jump.

Husky Bum can be played by just two people, one against the wall and one jumping. This version is sometimes known as 'Bugs'. Instead of holding up either a finger or thumb, a number of fingers can be held up instead, with the jumping player asking 'How many bugs?'. In some places the question was 'Finger, thumb or dum?', 'dum' being a clenched fist.

The game has some picturesque alternative names, including 'Finger, Thumb or Rusty Bum?', 'Husky Fusky', 'Jump the Nagger', 'Jeremiah', 'Montykitty' and 'Ton Weights'. In a version called 'Hi Jimmy Knacker', there is no rhyme; in order to win, the mounted team must remain seated for a certain length of time without being dislodged.

The game is probably centuries old; a similar activity is depicted in *Children's Games*, a 1560 painting by the Flemish artist Pieter Brueghel the Elder. But these days Husky Bum and Hi Jimmy Knacker seem to have vanished from our streets and playgrounds, probably banned for being too dangerous, a concern that in this case seems justified.

I Sent a Letter to My Love

Hanky Panky

This energetic game is best played by a group of twelve or more. Everyone stands in a circle. The player chosen to be It is given a handkerchief or scarf and runs round the outside of the circle singing or saying the following rhyme:

> I sent a letter to my love
> And on the way I dropped it.
> One of you has picked it up
> And put it in your pocket.

The other players are not allowed to look behind them. At some point, It drops the handkerchief stealthily behind one of the other players and then races around the outside of the circle as fast as they can. The player left with the hanky – assuming they have noticed it – must quickly pick it up and race around the circle in the opposite direction. The first person to make it back to the empty space is the winner. The loser becomes the next player to drop the handkerchief.

An easier version for younger children omits the handkerchief and uses the following rhyme to make it more obvious who is being chosen:

> A tisket, a tasket,
> A green and yellow basket,
> I wrote a letter to my love
> And on my way I dropped it,
> I dropped it, I dropped it,
> And on my way I dropped it.
> Somebody here has picked it up
> And put it in your pocket.

It isn't you; it isn't you;
It's YOU!

As It moves around the circle, they tap each player on the back in turn until they say the words 'It's YOU!'. They can prolong the moment of selection by repeating the words 'It isn't you' for as long as they like.

In a version known as 'Dummy', the loser must stand in the centre of the circle and suck their thumb; this punishment is sometimes also meted out to the handkerchief dropper if they are caught, or to a player who does not spot that the handkerchief has been dropped behind them until the dropper has run once round the circle.

In a closely related version called 'Duck, Duck, Goose' or – more exotically – 'Zebra, Zebra, Tiger', the person chosen to be It walks around the outside of the circle saying 'Duck' each time they tap someone on the shoulder. Eventually, It says 'Goose' instead and the player who has been called 'Goose' must jump up and race It back to the empty space in the circle. Whoever loses becomes It in the next round.

Sometimes less imaginatively known as 'Drop Handkerchief' and 'Filling the Gap', the game has also gone by the names of 'Allicomgreenzie' and 'Hunting a Deer in My Lord's Park', which implies a medieval origin. I Sent a Letter to My Love transports us back to the days when smitten young men would give love tokens to their maiden of choice. Indeed, a version called 'Kiss in the Ring' was played throughout the 19th century at Christmas and midsummer festivities, as well as at weddings and fairs. A girl would choose a boy standing in the circle, or a boy one of the girls. A chase around the outside of the ring would ensue, and if the pursuer caught the pursued, they both went into the middle and exchanged a kiss.

I Spy
I Spy, with My Little Eye ...

I Spy is the classic game of last resort for parents to play with bored children. It is amazing the distraction such a simple game can provide but its simplicity lends it adaptability and it can be played anywhere and any time (except perhaps on a dark night). It has the advantage of honing both the powers of observation and the letter-learning of young players.

One player chooses an object that they can see and says 'I spy, with my little eye, something beginning with ...', completing the sentence with the first letter of the name of the object. The other players take it in turns to guess what the object is. The player who guesses correctly is the next person to take a turn at spying.

I Spy is commonly played on car journeys, the only complication being that spied objects such as cows and postboxes have a tendency to disappear from view. In this case, the person who has chosen the I Spy might say something like 'Can't see it any more. Now I can!' to avoid long and frustrating periods of fruitless guessing.

For children too young to be well versed in the letters of the alphabet, colours can be used instead. 'I spy, with my little eye, something that is red' (that will be the postbox again ...). To make the game more difficult, the 'spy' does not reveal the first letter of the object; instead players guess the object by asking questions that may only be answered with 'yes' or 'no'. So players might ask 'Is it alive?', 'Does it move?' or 'Is it red?'.

The game of I Spy inspired a series of little spotters' guides on scores of different subjects, such as birds, flowers, inn signs and trains; these were launched in the 1950s at

pocket-money prices and are still available today. The pocket-sized paperback books contain pictures of objects that might be spotted 'On a Car Journey' or 'By the Seaside', with a box next to each object so it can be ticked off once it has been seen. Points are awarded for each object spotted according to how relatively rare it is. Players need 1,000 points to send off for the coveted I Spy badge. Children are extremely honest when applying for the badge about what they have seen with their own eyes – claims to have seen a golden eagle or the Eddystone Lighthouse when really they live in central London are very rare.

The I Spy books were a godsend to parents, enabling children to play without their input; the game tends to pall more quickly for adults than for children. But by the time players become bored with it, playing will have killed time entertainingly, which after all is the whole point.

Jacks
Stones and Bones

The game of Jacks was all the rage during the 1950s and 1960s, when children could often be seen clutching a little cloth bag that contained a number of jacks and a small rubber ball. The jacks themselves are small metal or plastic six-pronged objects shaped like three-dimensional crosses, or sputniks, to use an appropriately late-1950s description.

At the start of a game the jacks are thrown onto the ground to scatter them about. The first player takes the ball and throws it up into the air. While the ball is in flight, the player quickly picks up one of the jacks and then catches the ball before it hits the ground. The jack that has been picked up is transferred to the other hand, so that another jack can be picked up after the ball has been thrown again, and so on, until all the jacks have been retrieved. In the next round, players must pick up two jacks each time, and then three at a time, and so on. If they miss or drop any jacks, they are out and it is the next player's turn.

An easier version allows players to let the ball bounce before catching it. Alternatively, a greater degree of difficulty can be added by inserting a clap of the hands or a slap of the knees before picking up the jacks and catching the ball.

Jacks is related to a number of similar games that have been played for thousands of years, and in as many locations as there are places to play. Examples include 'Jackstones', 'Chuckstones', 'Dibs', 'Dabs', 'Gobs', 'Otadama', 'Tally' and 'Knucklebones'.

Knucklebones is a particularly ancient forerunner of Jacks. Traditionally played with the knucklebones of an animal, usually a sheep, it was known to the ancient Greeks, with references to a game of this kind occurring in both the *Odyssey* and the *Iliad*. Knucklebones was also widely played in Roman times.

Another common name for the game is 'Five Stones', as it can be played just as easily with small smooth stones picked up from the ground. Some people played the game using shop-bought ceramic, coloured cubes that came in

Jacks

a little box and are still sold today.

In Knucklebones and Five Stones, no ball is involved. Instead, the five stones or bones are thrown up in the air and the player must catch as many as possible on the back of their hand. The stones the player catches are then thrown up again from the back of the hand, and caught in the palm of the same hand. If no stones are caught, that player's turn is over.

However, if the player succeeds in catching at least one stone, they throw all of the stones except one onto the ground in preparation for the next go. They then throw the single stone in the air, pick up another stone from the ground and catch the stone they threw, all with one hand. This process is repeated until all the stones have been picked up. As with Jacks, in the next round they must pick up two stones at a time ('twos'), then three ('threes') and so on.

One of the most delightful aspects of this antique game are the terms that have been coined for the various throwing challenges invented by its players. These include 'horse in the stable', 'playing golf', 'camels', 'through the arch', 'riding the elephant', 'pigs in the sty', 'catching flies', 'cut the cabbage' and 'my pussy-cat likes fresh milk'.

None of us could throw spillikins in so perfect a circle, or take them off with so steady a hand. Her performances with cup and ball were marvellous. The one used at Chawton was an easy one, and she has been known to catch it on the point above a hundred times in succession, till her hand was weary.

So wrote Jane Austen's nephew James Edward Austen-Leigh, In a memoir of his aunt written after her death in 1817. The ivory cup and ball he mentions can still be seen in the museum in Jane Austen's former home at Chawton in Hampshire, along with a set of whalebone spillikins. Both look impossibly delicate when compared with today's sturdy plastic playthings but they clearly survived a great deal of use.

Jane had a largely unclouded country rectory childhood, and with four older brothers there was probably a lot of rough and tumble. Perhaps her own memories of such play inspired the passage in *Northanger Abbey* where she describes the tomboyish childhood of her heroine, Catherine Morland, also the daughter of a country clergyman:

She was fond of all boys' plays, and greatly preferred cricket, not merely to dolls, but to the more heroic enjoyments of infancy ... she was moreover noisy and wild, hated confinement and cleanliness, and loved nothing so well in the world as rolling down the green slopes at the back of the house.

When they grew out of such sport, the Austen children »

The Novelist at Play

» entertained themselves by putting on theatrical productions in the barn in the field across the road from the rectory, some of them scripted by Jane herself.

As an adult, Jane Austen clearly maintained her prowess at Spillikins and at cup and ball. Such skills must have come in handy, for although childless herself, she acquired 24 nephews and nieces courtesy of her married brothers. She reports in one letter that she has been playing at Battledore

and Shuttlecock with her nephew William, a game in which two people hit a shuttlecock between them with bats known as battledores as many times as possible without allowing it to hit the ground.

He & I have practised together two mornings, & improve a little; we have frequently kept it up three times, & once or twice six.

William and his aunt clearly needed to keep practising; in 1830, the Somerset family reportedly managed 2,117 hits.

When her brother Edward lost his wife shortly after she gave birth to her eleventh child in 1808, Aunt Jane was on hand to help console two of his other children, 14-year-old Edward and 12-year-old George. They came to stay with her, and she diverted them from their grief by playing Bilbocatch (an anglicized version of *bilboquet*, the French name for cup

and ball), Spillikins, riddles, conundrums and card games, making paper ships and going for walks along the river.

While I write now, George is most industriously making and naming paper ships, at which he afterwards shoots with horse chestnuts.

Jane wrote to her sister Cassandra.

'Aunt Jane' was clearly just the sort of grown-up that children like most: energetically at play even as an adult and entering with gusto into whatever fun was to be had.

Kerb or Wall
Bricking It

Kerb is a fast and furious street game, once played by urchins everywhere. Its rules make it particularly suited to the narrow terraced streets that once characterized large areas of northern industrial towns, although any street bounded by walls or even hedgerows does just as well.

One player is chosen to be It, usually by means of a dipping rhyme. The rest of the players line up against a wall and hold out their hands. The player who is It walks along the line, slapping each hand in turn while repeating one of the rhymes that seem to be unique to this game:

> *Two little dicky birds*
> *Sat upon a wall.*
> *One named Peter*
> *The other named Paul.*
> *Paul said to Peter,*
> *Peter said to Paul,*
> *Let's have a game*
> *At Kerb and Wall.*

or

> *Bim, bam, boo and a wheezy anna,*
> *My black cat can play the piano,*
> *One, two, three, kick him up a tree,*
> *Kerb or wall?*

or

> *Peter Pan said to Paul,*
> *Who do you like the best of all,*
> *Kerbstone, or the solid brick wall?*
> *Said Peter Pan to St Paul,*
> *Who lives at the bottom of the garden wall?*

The last person whose hand is slapped must choose Kerb or Wall. If he chooses Kerb, he must run as fast as possible to the edge of the nearest kerb and back to the wall where he started, then across the road to the far wall and back to his own wall again. If he chooses Wall, he must run first to the far wall and back to his own wall, then to the near kerb and back. The person who is It does the opposite, so that if Kerb is chosen, It must do Wall, and vice versa. Whoever wins the race becomes It in the following round, and selects a new opponent.

The race often results in players tripping up or bashing into walls at speed, and grazes and bruises are normal side-effects of the game.

Kim's Game
Memories are Made of This

Kim's Game is a memory-testing game that takes its name from Rudyard Kipling's eponymous novel *Kim*, the story of an orphan boy who grows up in India and is trained for government intelligence work. His initiation begins when Mr Lurgan, a dealer in jewellery and other curiosities who also works for the Intelligence Service, shows him a tray of precious stones and gems for one minute before covering it. Kim is then asked to recall the details of each stone, to test his powers of observation. At first he can remember only a few of the objects, but with practice he is able not only to name them all but also to describe them accurately.

Kim's Game found a champion in Robert Baden-Powell, the founder of the Scouting movement and a friend of Kipling's, who described the exercise in his book *Scouting Games*.

At birthday parties in the 1970s, Kim's Game was more often known as 'Things on a Tray'. Mum would arrange a selection of perhaps 10 to 15 common objects – buttons, scissors, cutlery, a pencil, a stone – on a tea tray and cover them with a cloth. The tray would then be carried through to the party room and the waiting guests, who were provided with pen and paper.

The cloth would be taken off the tray for 30 seconds or, more generously, one minute to give everyone time to memorize the objects; during this time no writing was allowed. Then the cloth would be replaced and there would follow a frenzy of grimacing and scribbling as everyone tried to remember all the items they had seen.

Kim's Game

After five minutes for thinking and writing, the objects were revealed once more and their names called out one by one. The player with the most correct objects on their list was declared the winner.

There are some entertaining variations on the game. In 'Flying Saucer Kim's Game', one person throws a selection of objects one by one across the room to another, who immediately places them in a bag. Players have to memorize the objects that have been thrown and list them on a piece of paper afterwards.

In 'Copycat Kim', the players are shown a selection of objects in the usual fashion. Once the objects are covered over, the players have to go in search of examples of the same objects and place them on a similar-sized tray or box in the same relative positions. Or there is 'Feeling Kim', in which the objects are placed in a bag and players are given one minute to feel around inside and memorize the objects they encounter.

Whatever the version, Kim's Game provides valuable exercise for the brain's grey matter in the guise of a popular party game – and especially for children who aspire to become a secret agent.

King of the Castle

But Not for Long!

Children lose few opportunities to lord it over their playmates by climbing up or onto things – walls, hills, trees – and calling out:

> *I'm the King of the Castle,*
> *You're the dirty rascals.*

This can be a simple taunt or the cue for a rough game in which the sneered-upon below attempt to push or drag the King down from his lofty perch or heap of earth. It is about making sure that no one, not even the King, gets the better of you. And that is really all there is to it.

The origin of the game of King of the Castle, or 'King of the Hill' as it is commonly known in North America, is lost in the mists of time. In his 1560 painting *Children's Games*, the Flemish artist Pieter Brueghel the Elder depicted a group of children playing King of the Castle. Perhaps the children of earlier ages were inspired to play it by personal experience of their local stronghold being besieged by marauders. The game is certainly inspired by and appeals to a basic instinct for survival that makes command of the high ground an advantage; even young animals, particularly frisky lambs, seem to play a similar game.

REVIVAL MEETING?
Games Deserving a Revival

While many party games have survived for centuries, others have fallen by the wayside and are rarely played now. Unusual the birthday party that does not include some of the old favourites: Pass the Parcel, Musical Chairs, Pin the Tail on the Donkey. But to ring the changes, why not revive some of the following?

Farmyards

Before the guests arrive, dried peas are hidden all around one or more rooms. The peas should all be clearly visible. The guests are divided into five or six groups with a captain for each, and each group is given the name of an animal, the cry of which the players have to imitate. The object of the game is for each group to find as many peas as possible but only the captain is allowed to pick them up. As soon as a player spots a pea, they must stand in front of it and make the appropriate animal call until the captain hears and rushes to collect the pea. The ensuing mayhem has to be heard to be believed.

King of the Cocks

All the players sit in a circle on the floor, and one player is chosen to be the King of the Cocks. The King of the Cocks stands in the middle and points to one of the players saying 'I am the King of the Cocks, and I want to fight with you'. The chosen player joins the King in the middle and they both bend over with their hands clasped round their knees, and then gently push each other until one topples over. The winning player becomes King of the Cocks in the next round.

Brother, Where Art Thou?

Two players are blindfolded and then lie full-length on the floor, in a straight line, head to head and face downwards. They grasp one another's left hands and keep the arms at full stretch. In their right hand, each holds a rolled newspaper. The first player begins by saying 'Brother, where art thou?'. His opponent replies 'Here'. The first player then tries to smite him with his rolled-up newspaper, making a downward (not sideways) sweep with it. Only one hit is allowed. Then the second player has a turn. Each player is allowed about ten blows and then someone else has a turn.

Scoop the Marbles

This game requires a large quantity of marbles, a large dish and a shoe horn. The object is to scoop up the marbles from a table or other surface and transfer them to the dish, which is placed some distance away, using only the shoe horn for the purpose: a task that is really rather difficult.

Bottle Fishing

This game requires a bottle with a narrow neck and two pieces of string, each about 2–3m long. In the middle of each length of string, make a loop that will fit comfortably over the neck of the bottle. Put the players into pairs and choose two pairs to start. Put the bottle in the centre of the room, and seat the players around it in the form of a cross. Each person should be about a metre away from the bottle, and partners should sit opposite one another. Each pair is given one of the lengths of string, with each player holding one of the ends. On a given signal, each pair must try to get the loop over the neck of the bottle before their opponents manage to do so. Just as the loop is sliding nicely into position, the other pair pulls its string and knocks their opponents' out of the way ... hours of harmless amusement!

Kiss Chase

The Thrill of the Catch

Kiss Chase is nothing more than a version of Tag with puckered lips. But its legendary status in the playground earns it an entry to itself, for while playing Kiss Chase many a schoolgirl crush has been born, many a schoolboy cheek has reddened and many cruel taunts have been doled out: as the rhyme goes, '[Janet] and [John]. Sitting in a tree. K-I-S-S-I-N-G'.

Kiss Chase – also known as 'Kiss Catch', 'Kiss Cats', 'KC' and 'Catchie Kissie' – is a childhood manifestation of that age-old struggle, the battle between the sexes. Two teams, one of girls and one of boys, take it in turns to chase and catch members of the other team. Instead of tagging by tapping, they must catch the player by kissing them. When everyone has been caught, the teams swap the roles of

pursuer and pursued. Players are sometimes allowed to hide but more often, particularly when younger children play, there is just a lot of chasing about the playground. The game is not about who can run faster or slower, as in standard versions of Tag, so much as the strength of each individual's desire to kiss the girl or boy they are pursuing.

For younger players, Kiss Chase is either a source of good, clean fun or a huge embarrassment. Looking back on their own childhoods, grown men are often adamant that they never played it, and certainly boys often show greater reluctance than girls to join in such sport. From around the age of twelve onwards, however, 'both sexes show a certain willingness for the game', as Iona and Peter Opie coyly put it. Sometimes cuddles are given as well as kisses, while in some parts of England an element of violence is introduced, with variants such as 'Kiss, Cuddle or Torture', 'Kiss, Kick or Torture' or 'Kiss, Prick or Torture' doling out alternatives such as hugs, well-aimed kicks or pricks with a pin when someone is caught.

Often the game is played under cover of darkness and away from prying and parental eyes. Then a peck on the cheek can easily segue into a snog. The number of people whose first 'proper' kiss resulted from a game of Kiss Chase should not be underestimated.

While the more prudish might feel that Kiss Chase is nothing but an invitation to promiscuity in the guise of a playground game, others will remember it as an innocent part of childhood, a way for boys and girls to show a partiality for one another long before the spectre of sex started to loom large in their lives.

Knock Down Ginger

Cold Calling

Rare the person who has not, at some point in their lives, been party to the childish trick of ringing on neighbourhood doorbells and then scarpering, leaving the startled resident to stand on the doormat and look up and down the road with a puzzled or exasperated expression.

The odd name of Knock Down Ginger is said to derive from the ginger-coloured paint once routinely used on the doors of houses on council estates. Usually played under cover of darkness, this prank – also known as 'Knock Knock Ginger', 'Ding Dong Ditch', 'Knock Door Run', 'Dolly Knock', 'Knock and Bomb' and 'Nicky, Nicky Nine Door' – is widespread and has many variations. These include:

- Knocky Nine Doors – the participants knock or ring on every ninth door and try to get to the end of the street before being caught or reprimanded.

- Sour Puss – the participants say 'Sour puss' or another predetermined phrase when their victim opens the door.

- All Doors – the participants ring and knock on all the doors of a house – front, back and sides – before running away.

- Knock and Don't Run – the participants ring the doorbell and stay put. The longer the victim keeps the door open, the more points the player gets.

- Gnoming – similar to Knock and Don't Run, but when the door opens the player must stand very still and if the

victim speaks to them, the player has to fall over. The player is only allowed to leave once the victim has gone back inside and closed the door.

- Knock Door ABC – participants knock on the door and then recite the alphabet while waiting for someone to answer. When the door is opened, the player asks for an imaginary person whose name must begin with whatever letter of the alphabet they had reached.

Home owners have been known to resort to spoiler tactics, such as taping a drawing pin, point side up, over the doorbell. Pranksters respond by devising ever more fiendish methods of attack, including using fishing line or cotton tied to door knockers to make possible long-distance harassment from a place of concealment. In a block of flats, tying two opposite door knockers together can also be highly effective. This particular technique also worked well in narrow streets of terraced houses, where several door knockers could be linked at once, thus setting off a chain reaction when one door was opened. Oh, the mischief!

Yes, the game of Knock Down Ginger is inane, juvenile, highly annoying and possibly enough of a nuisance to justify a phone call to the local constabulary. But there are few games that induce so much mirth in the perpetrators, and although it might be remembered with shame, most people will sheepishly admit to having played Knock Down Ginger at least once in their childhood.

Ladder of Legs
Fancy Footwork

This is an exciting and energetic activity that calls for unflinching bravery on the part of the participants. The more players the better, but the game does require a lot of space so it is best played outside or in a large hall.

The players are divided into two teams, and the teams sit on the floor facing one another with their legs stretched out. Each player sits directly opposite a member of the other team, so that the soles of their feet are touching. A gap should be left between each pair of players and there needs to be plenty of space behind each line. Each pair of players is given a number.

The game starts with one of the numbers being called out at random. The pair of players with that number scramble to their feet and run down the middle of the ladder of legs, leaping over the outstretched limbs until they reach the top of the line. Then they run behind their teammates to the bottom of the line and up the ladder from the other end until they reach their original places once more. The first player back wins and gains a point for their team. The game ends when every player has had a turn running down the ladder. The team with the most points is the winner.

The game becomes more exciting, not to say hazardous, if two numbers are called out at once. Older players might enjoy the greater intellectual challenge of 'Chinese Ladders', in which a simple arithmetical question is called out instead of a number. The answer to the sum is the number of the pair who must get up and negotiate the ladder.

As an alternative to numbers, each pair of players can be given the name of a different colour, fruit, animal, flower, pop band, football team, etc. Or each pair can be given the name of an object in a story – about a shopping trip, say, or a journey around the town – which they must listen out for and react to as the story is related.

And the unflinching bravery? That is required of the players in the ladder who are *not* running, if their speeding teammates lack the coordination or accuracy of aim to avoid trampling on their outstretched legs. Seated players must also take care to keep their hands close to their bodies to prevent fingers falling victim to galloping feet. Heavy shoes are not really suitable footwear for playing this game; trainers or even bare feet are preferable.

Leapfrog
Up and Over

Children have probably played Leapfrog as long as children have been leaping anywhere. They certainly played it in the time of the Flemish painter Pieter Brueghel the Elder, as his 1560 painting *Children's Games* shows a group of boys engaged in a game. And Shakespeare's Henry V describes himself to Princess Katherine, his future queen, as more warrior than courtier, declaring: 'If I could win a lady at leapfrog ... I should quickly leap into a wife'.

To play Leapfrog, the Frog gets into position by bending over and grasping their ankles. For younger children, the Frog could also kneel on the ground to present a lower target. The Leaper takes a running jump and vaults over the Frog, pushing down on the bent back and springing with the feet to take themself over. The satisfying sensation of timing a leap just right is quickly followed by the sinking feeling with which a Leaper bends over to become the Frog, hoping they will not collapse or get a kick in the head (the secret is to keep the head well tucked in). Frogs can stand either sideways on, or with their bottoms presented to the Leapers. As yet, there have been no scientific studies to establish which is the safer of the two positions.

Leapfrog can be played by two people taking it in turns to leap over one another. It is even more fun with a bigger group although it requires more organization. Everyone lines up. The first player in the line bends down and the second leaps over him, takes a few steps forward and bends down to become a Frog. The third in line jumps over these two players and then makes another Frog, and so on. When everyone in the line has had a turn at leaping and crouching, the player who became the first Frog leaps over all the others.

In a more fast and furious version of this, sometimes known as 'Keep the Kettle Boiling', more than one person can leap at a time, which means that the leading Leaper has to be quick to bend over on reaching the head of the line of Frogs. In this way the game can continue until everyone falls over or gets bored.

Leapfrog can also be played in two teams, one team starting as the Frogs and the other as the Leapers, and then swapping over. In this competitive version it is common for the Frogs to jiggle around or dip down suddenly in an attempt to throw a Leaper off balance. In 'Higher and Higher', the Frogs make their backs a little higher each time. If a player is unable to make the required leap they must drop out. In this way, players are eliminated until a winning team is decided.

In an interesting variant known as 'Spanish Leapfrog', an object is placed on the back of the person who bends over into the Frog position. The other players must leap over the Frog's back without dislodging the object. Anyone who fails to leap clear becomes the Frog.

Surprisingly, the game is known not as Leapfrog in France, but as *le saute-mouton*, a name that translates rather nicely as 'leap sheep'.

AMUSING 'THE YOUTH OF GREAT BRITAIN'
Games of the 1830s

Our plan embraces the amusements of all minds, and of all seasons, – in winter and in summer, – at home and abroad; the robust and the delicate, – the contemplative and the ingenious, – have each their tastes provided for.

So promised the compilers of *The Boy's Own Book*, published in the early 1830s and dedicated to 'The Youth of Great Britain'. And it is indeed very comprehensive. These amusements, both charming and less than charming, included:

Sports with Toys
- The Pop-gun
- The Sling
- The Pea-shooter

Miscellaneous Sports
- Sliding
- Skating
- The Snow Statue (a snowman which, once constructed, is immediately demolished by throwing snowballs at it)

The Fancier
- Singing Birds (with instructions on how to trap them)
- Silkworms ('the rearing of silkworms is an agreeable and interesting pursuit for young persons')
- Rabbits
- Guinea Pigs
- White Mice
- Pigeons
- Bantams

Arithmetical, Magnetic, Optical and Chemical Amusements
- The Sovereign and the Sage (a fiendish mathematical puzzle)
- The Horsedealer's Bargain (an equally fiendish mathematical puzzle)
- The Miraculous Dial (a complicated trick with a magnetic dial and an empty clock case)
- The Intelligent Fly (a fortune-telling trick)
- The Camera Obscura
- The Magic Lantern
- Sympathetic Ink (experiments with invisible inks)

- The Exploding Taper (relighting a taper by plunging it into a jar of oxygen)

The Conjuror

- Legerdemain (sleight of hand)
- Tricks with Cards
- Artificial Fireworks

Miscellaneous Recreations

- Deaf and Dumb Alphabet (a form of sign language)
- Paradoxes and Puzzles
- The Riddler

Perhaps most entertaining of all are the Conundrums. Choice examples from the 130 listed include:

Why are children at the breast like soldiers on a campaign?

They are both in arms

Why should boiled peas of a bad colour be sent to Knightsbridge?

It is the way to Turnham Green.

Why does the eye resemble a schoolmaster in the act of flogging?

It has a pupil under the lash.

Why is a handsome woman like bread?

She is often toasted.

Why should ladies' wet linen remind us of going to church?

The belles are wringing.

And what of 1830s' girls? They had their own reference work: 'Price One Guinea, Splendidly Bound in Embroidered Crimson Silk, "THE YOUNG LADY'S BOOK": a complete repertory of every graceful and improving pursuit, exercise, and accomplishment'. Not a pea-shooter in sight, however.

Marbles
Knuckle Down

Marbles must be one of the most attractive games ever invented: rare the child who has not thrilled to the possession of a bag of glass balls in gorgeous swirly colours clicking against one another. Additions to one's collection are always keenly coveted, and many a precious toy has been sacrificed in the swap for a particularly dazzling new marble.

Marbles is as old as it is aesthetically pleasing. It is thought to have been played in ancient Egypt and in Roman times, and children in Britain have been participating in marble contests for at least 400 years. Marbles come in a myriad sizes and colours, and as the name suggests, were originally sometimes made from bits of marble. However, they were also made from clay, stone, agate and glass, as they are today.

So universal a game is marbles that it has many different names. In England, the game is known variously as 'Marleys', 'Commoneys', 'Stoneys' and 'Potteys'. Some marbles were made of alabaster, and particularly coveted; such prized specimens were called 'alleys'. The marble used for shooting is a 'taw' or 'shooter'.

Hundreds of games can be played with marbles, and players often invent their own, but more organized versions tend to fall into three main categories: circle games, hole games and chase games.

The most basic marble game is a circle game, 'Ringer' or 'Ring Taw', in which marbles have to be struck out of a circle marked on the ground. The circle may be between three feet and ten feet in diameter; the larger the circle, the more difficult the game. Thirteen 'mibs' or 'ducks' (slightly smaller marbles than the shooters) are placed in the centre of the circle, either in the shape of an X or in another circle. Each player tries to knock one or more of the mibs out of the circle without their shooter also going out; a point is gained for every mib that is knocked out. A successful shot allows a player to shoot again from the place where the shooter landed. If they miss the mibs, their opponent takes a turn; if the shooter lands outside the circle, the player must start again. Players may also try to knock their opponent's shooter out of the circle. Play continues until all the mibs have been knocked out; the player with the most points wins.

The most competitive games of marbles generally involve 'keepsies'. This means that players get to keep any of their opponent's marbles that they strike out of the ring.

Hole games involve shooting the mibs into some kind of opening. The hole can be in the centre of the sort of circle described above, or several holes placed some distance apart from one another into which the marbles must be shot in sequence.

In chase games, players take it in turns to shoot at their opponent's marbles. In the simplest version, sometimes known as 'Spanners', one player rolls a marble and the other player tries to hit it. If he succeeds, he keeps it. If he misses, the other player has a shot, and so on. If a player loses a marble, he must produce another from his precious hoard to stay in the game. The version sometimes referred to as 'Plunkers' is played on the hoof –

on the way to school, for example. Players roll their marbles as far ahead as they want, aiming at any other marbles in front of them. A marbles game similar to bowls or boules can also be played in which smaller marbles are aimed at a larger 'jack' marble.

Chasing marble games were sometimes played in the gutter as this helped to contain the marbles. Drain covers could also be used, with each player taking turns to flick their marble so it would stop on the same 'bar' as someone else's marble. Unsurprisingly, many marbles were lost to the sewer system in this way.

The correct way to propel a marble is to balance it in the crook of a bent forefinger, with the thumb placed behind it for support. The hand is held close to the ground (usually while the player is in a kneeling position), the marble aimed and the thumb flicked sharply forward to fire the marble at the target. Players must have at least one knuckle on the ground when flicking; a player loses his turn if he should happen to 'fudge' or 'hist', ie lift his hand completely off the ground as he shoots.

Marbles

'Lagging' decides which player takes the first shot in a game of marbles. A 'lag' line is drawn, towards which the players roll their marbles. Whoever gets closest to the line without actually going over it is awarded the first go.

It takes hours of practice to become proficient at marbles. Happy the player who leaves the field of combat triumphantly bearing new glass trophies to add to his collection. But cruel the fate of those who lose prized treasures under the rule that winners are keepers.

May I?
Politeness Itself

This endlessly inventive game, also known as 'Mother, May I?', 'Captain, May I?' and 'Walk to London', is played by children all over the country.

One player is chosen to be the Caller and stands some distance away from the other players and facing them. The Caller invites one of the players to make a number of moves towards her in a certain style. For example, she might say 'Take two bunny hops' or 'Do one cartwheel'.

Before the selected player complies with the request, they must ask 'May I?'. Only when consent is granted by the Caller are they allowed to proceed. If they forget to say 'May I?' they have to go back to the start. It then becomes the turn of the next player, who is given a different sequence of moves to make but must also remember to ask 'May I?' before they start. The winner of the game is the first player to reach the Caller, and the winner becomes the Caller for the next round.

These deceptively simple rules underlie a wealth of possible moves that are particular to this game. Dozens of moves have been documented, but among the most widely known are:

Baby Step take a small heel-to-toe step (also known as a Dolly or Fairy Step).

Banana Slip slide one foot forward as far as possible and bring the other up behind it.

Barrel spin round and move forward at the same time.

Bucket link both hands and then bend down and step over them.

Caterpillar move forward while lying face down on the

ground, by pulling up the knees and pushing the body forward.

Cup and Saucer take one big jump forward from a crouching position, followed by one jump with the legs apart.

Giant Step take as long a stride as possible.

Lamp Post lie down on the ground, stretch both arms out as far as possible and then go to stand on the spot your fingertips reached.

Pigeon Step take a step the length of your foot.

Scissors take a jump forward with the feet apart, then another jump with the feet together.

Squashed Tomato the player runs towards the Caller with both arms crossed in front of the body. The Caller runs towards the player at the same time. The point where the two run into one another is the place the player advances to.

Umbrella twirl around on one foot with arms extended and take a step forward with the other foot when the turn is completed.

Watering Can spit as far as possible and then go to stand where the spit lands.

The pleasure of playing May I? lies not only in the competitive element but also in watching the other players making a spectacle of themselves as they attempt ever more complicated sequences of moves. Frustration arises from becoming so distracted by this that you forget to ask permission when your own turn comes and then have to start all over again.

Murder in the Dark

Game Noir

Murder in the Dark is a perennially popular pursuit with young people as it involves utter mayhem, complete with blood-curdling screams, dramatic death-throe sound effects and many a spine-chilling encounter in pitch darkness. It is also the ideal game for those who fancy themselves as Sherlock Holmes.

The rules are elementary. First, folded slips of paper are put into a hat, one slip for each player. One of the slips is marked with an X and another with a circle. Each player draws a slip of paper. The player who draws the X is the Murderer but keeps this fact to themselves. The player who draws the circle is the Detective and must make their role known to the others.

Everyone except the Detective disperses around the house as if they were playing Hide and Seek but without actually hiding. The lights are turned out and the Murderer sets off in search of a victim. When a suitable victim is encountered, the Murderer grabs them and whispers 'You're dead', whereupon the victim must emit a high-pitched scream and expire noisily. The Murderer flees before the Detective, having heard the scream (and how could he fail to), switches the lights back on and rushes to the scene of the crime. Everyone else stays exactly where they were when they heard the scream; the murder victim plays dead on the floor.

After viewing the body, the Detective begins his questioning of the Suspects. Everyone must answer truthfully apart from the Murderer, who is permitted to tell whopping lies in answer to any question except 'Are you the Murderer?'. The Detective watches everyone's face during the cross-examination, which can feature such Hercule Poirot favourites as 'Where were you, Mademoiselle, at the time of the murder?'. Once the Detective has completed the questioning, they are permitted three guesses to the identity of the Murderer. If the Detective fails to discover the culprit, the Murderer gleefully owns up.

Murder in the Dark can also be played with a pack of cards. Remove three Kings and three Aces from the pack and deal out the remaining cards to the players. Whoever holds the Ace in their hand is the Murderer; the holder of the King is the Detective.

In a different version, the Murderer is allowed to kill as many people as they want before the lights go on again by tapping them on the shoulder. The victims fall to the ground, with whatever dramatic sound effects they wish to produce. If other players hear a murder being committed, they do not have to wait for the Detective but should shout 'Murder in the Dark' as loudly as possible and reach for the light switch themselves.

NORTH OF THE BORDER
A Miscellany of Scottish Names and Rhymes

Hopscotch is known as 'Peevers' or 'Beds'.

Ha, ha, ha, hee, hee, hee,
Can't catch me for a bumble bee.
(taunt)

'Here I come, ready or not, if ye're spied it's no my fau't' – words said at the beginning of a game of Hide and Seek.

Mrs McGuire peed on
the fire.
The fire was too hot;
She sat on a pot.
The pot was too wide;
She sat in the Clyde.
And all the wee fishies
ran up her backside.
(skipping rhyme)

'Scotch and English' is a version of Capture the Flag that evokes a time of regular raids across the border: 'Here's a leap into thy land, thieving Sassenach'.

Eettle ottle,
Black bottle,
My dog's deid.
(dipping rhyme)

'Carly Doddies' is a duelling game similar to conkers but played with flower stalks; the first person to strike the flower off the other player's stalk is the winner.

Out goes a bonny lass, out goes she,
Out goes a bonny lass, one, two, three.
(dipping rhyme)

Het – a common term for the person who is It or On.

Eachie, peachie, pearie, plum,
Throw the tatties up the lum.
Santa Claus got one on the bum,
Eachie, peachie, pearie, plum.
(dipping rhyme)

Skin the Cuddy – the Scottish name for Hi Jimmy Knacker.

Musical Chairs
Sit Yourself Down

What children's birthday party is complete without a game of Musical Chairs? The game is a perennial favourite at parties across the world and goes by a variety of names. In Dutch it is known as 'Chair Dance', and in Japanese as the 'Game of Stolen Chairs'. The appeal seems to be lost on Russian children, however, as they call the game 'It's Boring Sitting Like This'!

Here's a reminder of how it works. Chairs are arranged in a straight line down the middle of the room, using one fewer chair than there are players. Alternate chairs should face in opposite directions. If there are not enough chairs available, cushions can be used instead.

Music is played and the players walk around the line of chairs – no dawdling or staying too close to the seats is allowed. When the music stops, everyone must sit down on the nearest available chair. The player who is left without a seat is out. At this point one chair is removed from the line and the music starts again. The game continues until only two players and one chair remain. The winner is the player who manages to sit on the last remaining chair when the music stops.

The game becomes even more exciting if a balloon is taped to each seat, as the players not only have to sit down but must burst the balloon as well. This has the advantage of settling the disputes that regularly arise because two players are jostling for the same seat; only the one who pops the balloon stays in the game.

The best-known variation on Musical Chairs is probably 'Musical Bumps'. In this version, the players walk or dance around the room and when the music stops they sit down

on the floor as quickly as possible. The last player to sit down is out. Play continues until only one player is left.

In 'Musical Statues', players move around the room until the music stops, when they must freeze immediately and stand without moving a muscle until the music starts again. Anyone judged to be wobbling or moving any part of their body is out. The game continues until only one player is left.

In 'Musical Clothes', a pile of clothes is placed in the middle of the room; there should be one fewer item of clothing than there are players. When the music stops, each player must put on one of the items of clothing; the player left with nothing to put on is out.

'Desert Islands' uses pieces of paper placed on the floor instead of chairs. When the music stops, each player must stand on one of the paper 'islands'. The player left without an 'island' is out.

In days gone by, Musical Chairs was commonly known as 'Going to Jerusalem' or 'The Trip to Jerusalem'. The name conjures up a holy, pilgrimage-like image that hardly seems in keeping with the game's self-seeking scramble for the last available seat in the house. The self-interest and competitiveness, though, make the game a perfect metaphor for the jockeying for position in politics, and indeed a game of Musical Chairs is used in the musical *Evita* to symbolize Juan Perón's rise to power.

Noughts and Crosses
X Marks the Spot

Who has not whiled away an idle moment or two in a game of Noughts and Crosses? It is a simple but mentally stimulating game that requires little equipment; a piece of paper and two pencils usually suffice, although the game has been played by scratching with sticks or other sharp objects on earth, sand and stone.

To play the game, draw out a grid of nine squares, with three squares to each row and column. One player is represented by a nought and the other by a cross. Players decide which of them will start the game and then take it in turns to mark either a nought or a cross in one of the squares until one player succeeds in making a straight line – vertical, horizontal or diagonal – of either three noughts or three crosses. The best squares to fill at the beginning are either the middle one or one of the corner squares, positions that increase the chances of completing a winning line.

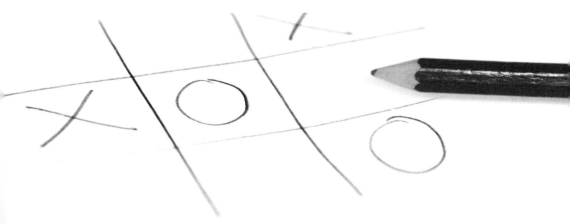

Mathematicians, intrigued by the game, have worked out that there are over 250,000 possible combinations, and that the player making the first mark is almost twice as likely to win as the player who goes second. Even so, it does not usually take novice players – even young children – long to learn how to scotch any potentially victorious moves. Consequently, and especially if both participants are canny players, many games end in a 'cat's game', or draw.

Variations on the game seek to make things more complicated. These include a three-dimensional version played on a board that is three squares wide by three squares deep by three squares high. Many other games, both ancient and modern, have exploited the same principle of making a winning line, including 'Nine Men's Morris', 'Connect 4' and 'Quarto'.

Noughts and Crosses is believed to be an ancient game. Remains of playing grids like those used for Noughts and Crosses have been found etched into surfaces all over the Roman empire's former territories, and some believe that the ancient Roman game of *terni lapilli* was an early version. None of the surviving grids of this game contains a single nought or cross, however, and it is thought that stones may have been used rather than nought and cross marks. The name *terni lapilli* supports this idea, as the Latin word *lapilli* refers to the small stones that fly through the air during a volcanic eruption, while *terni* is Latin for sets of three. But no-one knows precisely how the game of this name was played.

Today the game of Noughts and Crosses is found all over the world, and goes by many alternative names. In the

USA and Canada, it is known as 'Tic, Tac, Toe', in Ireland as 'Boxin' Oxen', in the Netherlands as 'Butter, Cheese and Eggs', in Brazil as 'Old Lady's Game' and in Norway as 'Farmer's Game'.

A version of Noughts and Crosses even became a television game show in the 1970s; *Celebrity Squares* sat well-known personalities in little boxes that appeared in a grid on-screen. The personalities – usually comedians and soap opera actors – had to answer questions correctly in order to fill the box with a nought or a cross and help that week's contestants on their way to a winning line.

If endless 'cat's games' of Noughts and Crosses begin to pall, try a *misère* version. In this, players try to *avoid* making a line of three while simultaneously trying to force their opponent into completing one. Not as easy as it sounds!

COME INTO MY PARLOUR
The Victorian Birthday Party

A child invited to a birthday party in a well-to-do household in late Victorian or Edwardian times would certainly put on their best bib and tucker. Perhaps a sailor suit if they were a boy, and if a girl, a white silk frock with a sash. Then they would sashay forth in great excitement, for in those days, the well-heeled birthday party offered an extensive programme of entertainment: music, dancing and recitations as well as games.

A party programme from the 1890s displayed at the Museum of Childhood in Bethnal Green, London, lists 36 separate elements. The afternoon began with the dancing of a Polka to get everyone in the party mood. Then the party-goers played a round of I Sent a Letter to My Love. Next there was a Duett [sic], followed by more dancing (a Waltz); a Mandoline Solo; a game of Nuts in May, and then a Recitation by Miss Ruthie Pratt. Other games played during the course of the party included Twos and Threes, Would You Know How? and Blind Man's Buff. After an Interval for Refreshments, there followed a Barn Dance, with such dances as the Sir Roger de Coverley. There must have been some very tired children going home after that particular party.

The Girl's Own Book by Mrs Child, published in 1864, lists many popular Victorian parlour games. For example, I Love My Love, in which each player takes a letter of the alphabet in turn, and must come up with an adjective or noun beginning with the appropriate letter to fill in the gaps in a rhyme:

I love my love with an A because he is Artless. I hate him with an A because he is Avaricious. He took me to the sign of the Anchor, and treated me to Apples and Almonds. His name is Abraham, and he comes from Alnwick.

Any hesitation or mistake is punishable by paying a forfeit or being eliminated from the game. Pity the poor player whose turn lands them with the letter X, although Mrs Child managed to come up with:

I love my love with an X because he is a Xylographer. I hate him with an X because he is a Xerophagian. He took me to the sign of the Xebec, and treated me to Xiphias-fish and Xeres wine. His name is Xavier, and he comes from Xalapa.

Hunt the Slipper was also popular, as were enigmas and riddles:

I have but one eye, and that without sight,
Yet it helps me, whatever I do;
I am sharp without wits, without senses I'm bright,
The fortune of some, and of some the delight,
And I doubt not I'm useful to you.
[Answer: A needle]

Mrs Child also mentions an entertainment called the Party Bag Game, in which a paper bag filled with sugar-plums is suspended from a door-frame or ceiling. Each of the guests is blindfolded in turn and given a stick with which they make three attempts to strike the bag. Eventually, the bag will tear and the sugar plums will fall onto the floor, whereupon all the children scramble for them. This diversion is remarkably similar to Piñata, a traditional Mexican game now popular at 21st-century birthday parties. For older children, Mrs Child suggests that the bag could be filled with 'little books, small pincushions, bodkins, beads and ribbon-yards'. She also proposes that the game is concluded by rigging up another bag which, unbeknown to the children, is filled with flour. So much for those best bibs and tuckers . . .

Number Games
Count Me In!

Just as alphabet games test spelling and verbal ingenuity, so number games test mental arithmetic and provide a mathematical workout for the brain.

Here are few to get the cogs whirring!

Fizz/Buzz

Here is one to help with those times tables! Players sit in a circle and begin counting round the circle in turn. But instead of saying the number seven or any multiple of seven, the player whose turn it is must say 'Fizz' instead. If they fail to do this on the correct number, they are out. To make things harder, the word 'Buzz' can be introduced as well to stand for multiples of a different number, for example eight. A number which is a multiple of both seven and eight, for example 56, should be called as 'Fizz Buzz'. Which number and multiples are chosen depends on which times tables need the most practice. For more advanced players, identifying prime numbers can be added.

Bingo

Possibly the most famous number game of all, this requires a degree of preparation. A number of grids are needed, each one containing a different random selection of numbers between 1 and 90; there should be between nine and twenty numbers in each grid. Then slips of paper, each marked with one of the numbers between 1 and 90, are placed in a hat. The bingo caller draws numbers from the hat and calls them out one by one. Each player has a grid and crosses off any number that appears in their own grid. As soon as a player has crossed out the last number in their grid, they call out 'House' and, if they are correct, they win a prize.

The main entertainment value in the game lies in 'bingo lingo', or the nicknames given to various numbers by the caller. Among the many are:

9 – doctor's orders

11 – legs eleven

16 – sweet sixteen

21 – key of the door

39 – those famous steps

76 – trombones

88 – two fat ladies

Time Bomb

All the players sit in a circle. The first player starts counting with either '1', '2' or '3'. The second player continues counting and can say either one, two or three additional numbers; for example, if the first player says '2', the second player can say '3', '3, 4' or '3, 4, 5'. Play continues around the circle until one player is forced to say '13'. That player is out!

Higher/Lower

This fun game has shades of the television show *The Price is Right*. One player thinks of a number and writes it secretly on a card, but in large bold writing that can be read from a distance. Two teams are formed, and one player is chosen from each. They stand up with their back to the person with the number who then holds it high in the air so that all the other players can see it. The players who cannot see the number take it in turns to say what they think the number is, and their teammates respond to the guess by saying 'Higher' or 'Lower'. This response, and the response to the number guessed by their opponent, helps them to adjust their next guess. Play continues until someone arrives at the right number. That team gains a point, and two different players take a turn at guessing.

Newspaper Sumo

Place a sheet of newspaper (preferably one from a broadsheet paper!) on the ground. Two players stand at each edge of the paper, facing away from one another. Each player takes it in turns to answer a mathematical question, for example 'What is 4×7?'. If they get the sum right, they take half a step backwards. Play continues until the two players' heels touch, at which point an almighty struggle ensues, as each player tries to push their opponent off the newspaper. The first player to touch any part of the ground wholly off the newspaper loses.

Number or Your Life

This game combines numbers and verbal reasoning, giving the players a rest from arithmetic.

Sitting in a circle, players take turns to call out any number up to and including 12. For each number, another player must call out a phrase or object with which that number is associated. Whichever player does this successfully gets a point. For example:

One – for the master; two, buckle my shoe; one is one and all alone and ever more shall be so.

Two – for tea; is company; little dicky birds.

Three – blind mice; little pigs; score years and ten.

Four – and twenty blackbirds; knock on the door.

Players may also call out numbers above 12 if they can make an association with that number, for example 60 – number of minutes in an hour; 100 – pence in a pound, and so on.

Nuts in May
A Seasonal Conundrum

This traditional singing game has fallen out of fashion but is still full of charm for those minded to play it.

The players divide into two teams of equal size and form two lines, facing one another across the room. Then a line is drawn down the middle of the space between the teams, or a marker (such as a length of string or a handkerchief) is put down.

The team chosen to start the game clasps one another's hands and walks up to the centre line and back again while singing (to the same tune as 'Here We Go Round the Mulberry Bush') the following:

> *Here we go gathering nuts in May,*
> *Nuts in May, nuts in May,*
> *Here we go gathering nuts in May*
> *On a cold and frosty morning.*

The other team responds by similarly moving forward and back, singing:

> *Who will you have for nuts in May,*
> *Nuts in May, nuts in May,*
> *Who will you have for nuts in May*
> *On a cold and frosty morning?*

The first group chooses a player from the second group (let's call her Jane) and replies:

> *We'll have Jane for nuts in May,*
> *Nuts in May, nuts in May,*
> *We'll have Jane for nuts in May*
> *On a cold and frosty morning.*

The second group then asks:

> *Who will you have to pull her away,*
> *Pull her away, pull her away,*
> *Who will you have to pull her away*
> *On a cold and frosty morning?*

The first team chooses one of its own players this time (let's call the lucky boy Jimmy) before singing:

> *We will have Jimmy to pull her away,*
> *Pull her away, pull her away,*
> *We will have Jimmy to pull her away*
> *On a cold and frosty morning.*

Jane and Jimmy come forward to stand either side of the middle line or marker. They then have a tug of war until one player loses by being pulled across to the opposing side. The losing player joins the winning team and the song is repeated until one side has lost all its players, or everyone has had enough.

The song seems to contain two unlikely ideas: that nuts could be gathered as early as May, when nuts do not ripen until the autumn; and that May mornings are likely to be cold and frosty. However, 'nuts' is believed to be a corruption of the word 'knots', the posies of flowers traditionally gathered to celebrate May Day and the end of winter. And 'May' is believed to refer not to the month but to the blossom of the hawthorn, which starts to flower in southern England from late March onwards, a time of year when frosty mornings are more likely. Substitute the words 'Here we go gathering knots of may' and the rhyme makes more sense.

Nuts in May

However, there is another theory about the nuts. Some believe that the song refers to the pignut, an edible plant tuber that was once widespread in British woodlands in spring. As well as providing a tasty meal for pigs – hence the name – pignuts were also foraged for and eaten by country folk. So the true original might have been 'Here we go gathering nuts *and* may'.

In some parts of Wales, the game of Tag is known as 'Tick'.

'Chain a Wedding' is a Welsh version of Chain Tag in which all the tagged players join hands until only one player is left, whereupon the chain breaks up to catch the untagged player. The first and last players to be caught become the chasing pair for the next game. Iona and Peter Opie thought that the name 'Chain a Wedding' may refer to the Welsh practice of stretching a rope across the road to obstruct a wedding procession and exacting a toll before the happy couple were allowed on their way.

> Please Mr Froggie may we cross
> the water
> To see the King's daughter
> To chuck her in the water
> To seem if she can swim?
> (rhyme accompanying a Welsh
> version of Please Mr Crocodile).

In *Nain Gogo* (or Grandmother Gogo), one player pretends to be dead or asleep on the ground and the other players creep up and prod or tickle her until suddenly she jumps up and tries to catch one of them. This game is also known in parts of Wales as 'Spider in the Corner'.

Bobby, Kick the Tin is an alternative name for Tin Can Tommy in Swansea.

Strange but true: the game of Grandmother's Footsteps or Peep Behind the Curtain is sometimes known as 'London' in Wales.

Oranges and Lemons
Peel and Peals

One of the most popular of children's singing games, Oranges and Lemons is also one of the oldest, dating from at least the 17th century.

Two children make an arch by joining hands and holding them high in the air, having first secretly decided which of them is to be Orange and which Lemon. The rest of the players walk or skip round and under the arch in a line, singing the song:

> *Oranges and lemons,*
> *Say the bells of St Clement's.*
> *You owe me five farthings,*
> *Say the bells of St Martin's.*
> *When will you pay me?*
> *Say the bells of Old Bailey.*
> *When I grow rich,*
> *Say the bells of Shoreditch.*
> *When will that be?*
> *Say the bells of Stepney.*
> *I'm sure I don't know,*
> *Says the great bell at Bow*
> *Here comes a candle to light you to bed,*
> *Here comes a chopper to chop off your head,*
> *Chop, chop, you're dead!*

As the song approaches its fateful last line, the arch is raised and lowered several times in a menacing way to warm up the chopper; even as adults, people remember this part as being quite terrifying. Finally, on the word 'dead', the arch is brought down to imprison one hapless

player. The prisoner must decide if they prefer to be an Orange or a Lemon and whisper their choice to the keepers of the arch. They are then told which of the two to stand behind, and the song begins again.

Once all the children have been 'chopped' and are standing in two lines, a tug of war is usual to decide whether the Oranges or the Lemons will prevail.

The song is said to represent the sound of the bells at different churches in the City of London. St Clement's church was near the fruit and vegetable markets of Cheapside and a wharf on the Thames where cargoes of citrus fruit were unloaded. St Martin's church is in an area of the city where moneylenders used to live, and the Old Bailey is not far from where the debtors' court and prison once stood at Newgate. The great bell of Bow is the one within the sound of which someone must be born to be a true Cockney.

The reference to the 'chopper' harks back to the age of public executions, when the bell of Old Bailey was rung to announce an imminent beheading. Thousands of people routinely turned out to watch the spectacle. Charles I was executed in 1649, a tumultuous event which might also have inspired the final lines. These rather sinister associations find an echo in George Orwell's novel *Nineteen Eighty-Four*, in which various characters struggle to remember all the lines of the song, their inability to do so symbolizing the near-complete eradication of their traditional culture by the propaganda of the totalitarian regime; the song is lost forever when the last people to remember all the words are dead.

Happily, the game and its song seem unlikely to suffer such a fate outside fiction, its bloodthirstiness being part of its perennial appeal for children even after 400 years.

Pass the Balloon
Fun to Bursting

There can be few party games to match Pass the Balloon for unbridled hilarity and general loss of decorum. Plenty of inflated balloons are needed to allow for the bedlam of bursting that is almost certain to result.

The players form two teams, which stand in parallel lines. The player at the front of each line is given a balloon and on the word 'Go', the teams pass the balloon as quickly as possible from person to person until it reaches the last person in the line.

Several techniques for passing the balloon can be used. In the simplest versions of the game, players may use their hands to pass the balloon but must follow a set sequence of moves, for example passing the balloon between the legs of one person and over the head of the next, and so on down the line.

Trickier but more entertaining versions prohibit the use of hands. The first player can start with the balloon either tucked under their chin or held between their knees. They must then employ whatever physical contortions are necessary to pass the balloon to the next player, either chin to chin or knee to knee.

The first team to pass the balloon to the end of the line wins. It is almost impossible to do this without cheating at some point, so some latitude is necessary on the part of the referee.

A relay version of the game is also popular. The first member of each team runs to get a balloon from the other end of the room, transporting it back to their team between

their knees. The team members then pass the balloon to the back of the line using only their knees. When the last player has the balloon, they must burst it and then sprint off to get another, returning to the front of the line this time. The process continues until the first player to have collected a balloon gets back to the front of the line. The first team to reach this point wins.

There are a number of passing games using alternative objects. 'Pass the Orange' or 'Necking the Orange' involves passing an orange tucked under the chin from one person to another. In 'Pass the Peanut' each team stands in a line holding hands, with a chair placed at either end of the line. On the chair at one end are ten peanuts and these must be passed one at a time from player to player until all are placed on the chair at the other end of the line. Sounds simple, but this must be accomplished while all the players keep their hands firmly clasped in one another's throughout. Another variation is a ping-pong race in which the two seated teams must pass a ping-pong ball from player to player along the line using only their outstretched feet.

LET'S PRETEND
Imaginative Games

Oh, the great pretenders that are children! Capable of creating entire make-believe worlds in the most ordinary of playgrounds or back gardens, they can imagine themselves promoted to players in the adult world – parents, soldiers, teachers, train drivers, kings and queens, pop stars, doctors, nurses – mimicking the adults around them, with their child's-eye view of what grown-ups do all day. Such games never seem to become boring, unlike the daily grind of adulthood.

Games of the imagination are played by both boys and girls, but with the exception of war games like Cops and Robbers and Cowboys and Indians, girls often take the lead, with boys being given walk-on parts at best.

There are no rules to imagination games, which is, of course, absolutely the point.

Mummies and Daddies
The most common role-playing game of all typically involves dolls and sometimes dressing up in oversized adult cast-offs. An area is designated as the house, marked out with rugs and blankets perhaps. In the traditional version, Daddy would invariably disappear to work at an early point in the game, while Mummy was left to sweep the floor, bath the baby and cook the tea (leaves, seeds and flower petals all making convincing victuals), which would naturally be on the table as soon as Daddy returned. One imagines that in more recent times, there have been some emancipated amendments to this scenario: Mummies and Childminders perhaps? Or Stay-at-Home Daddies?

Doctors and Nurses
To play at hospitals it is usual for at least one player to recline on the floor in the role of patient, and the other to administer treatment, whether a spoonful of medicine or bandages to the affected area. Ambulance noises are also de rigueur. Alternatively, a whole waiting list of dolls can be lined up ready to receive treatment. Games of Doctors and Nurses often provide children with a certain amount of anatomical knowledge of the opposite sex, acquired during the

thorough examinations that are necessary for diagnosis.

Horses

Cantering round the playground making neighing noises and blowing out the lips is perfectly normal girl behaviour, particularly for those who are mad about horses. To play horses and riders, a skipping rope can be looped around the girl playing the horse to make very effective reins. Tally ho!

Schools

Playing at schools gives children the very pleasurable chance to be the one who metes out homework, tellings-off and punishments instead of being on the receiving end. The role of Teacher is particularly suitable for bossier children, who love to organize their playmates into lines, give them work to do, and send them to stand in the corner

**You in a garden green
With me were king and
  queen,
Were hunter, soldier, tar,
And all the thousand
  things that children are.**

Robert Louis Stevenson

or to the Head if they do not behave. Once again, dolls and teddies can be substituted for real pupils; they are, after all, less likely to answer back!

Imaginative play is not confined to trying on different roles for size; it can also transform inanimate objects. A large cardboard box provides hours of fun, particularly indoors on a rainy day, when it might become a car, a boat, a train, a spaceship or other means of conveyance. A sheet or blanket draped over the kitchen table, with cushions inside, makes a cosy house or tent. A couple of chairs or even a clothes horse might be drummed into service indoors as an alternative to the table; outside, the sheet can be thrown over a washing line and weighed down at the edges with stones. How many children's first experience of 'camping' was under an old army blanket in the back garden?

Encouraging children to use their imagination when playing makes sense for adults too. Why buy lots of expensive toys when you can get away with providing an unwanted cardboard box, a clothes line and a hairy old blanket?

Pass the Parcel

When the Music Stops

No children's birthday party has ever been or ever could be complete without a round or two of Pass the Parcel. Whether it is the austerity or environmentally friendly version (ie layers of newspaper, and no consolation prizes between the layers), the rot-your-teeth version (packets of sweets between every layer) or the full-on luxury version (real wrapping paper and a proper gift between every layer), the invitation to play Pass the Parcel is guaranteed to get everyone sitting to attention.

The parcel must, in true *Blue Peter* fashion, be prepared earlier. The prize is wrapped in layer upon layer of paper until the parcel is large, squashy and immune to being dropped or thrown; if consolation prizes are included, they are inserted at intervals between the layers. Astonishingly, ready-made parcels with pre-packed layers can now be purchased, an innovation frowned upon by the budget-conscious and by those who consider the staging of children's parties to be a fine art.

When all the children are sitting on the floor in a circle, the parcel is handed to one of them and the music starts. The children pass the parcel round the circle – with the help of reminding nudges from supervising grown-ups if they get distracted, or hold the parcel too long in a deliberate attempt to fix the game. When the music stops, the child holding the parcel removes a layer of wrapping. Excitement mounts as the parcel gets smaller, until in the final round one lucky child unwraps the main prize.

The grown-up in charge of stopping and starting the music needs consummate timing and a good memory, for they must ensure that each child has a turn at unwrapping at least one layer, and that the eventual winner is not the birthday girl or boy, however unpopular that might be with the over-excited little darling.

The game can progress too slowly for small children if there is a large number of them, but boredom can be prevented by having two parcels, each circulating in a different direction. For older players, challenges or forfeits can be inserted between the layers to liven up the proceedings and make the game last longer. Or messages can be written on the outside of each layer, along the lines of 'Pass the parcel to the player on your left/the oldest player/the player with the longest hair'. Then when the music stops, the player holding the parcel must obey the instruction and hand over the parcel for someone else to open.

However, so tried and tested and so universally recognized is the game that there is little need for variations. The only hazards are children who throw a tantrum when they do not get a present, and power cuts; in the latter case you can always sing.

Piggy in the Middle

Butterfingers Beware

Piggy in the Middle is usually a game for three players. Two people throw a ball to each other while a third player – the Piggy – stands in between them and tries by jumping to intercept the ball in mid-flight. If the Piggy succeeds in catching the ball, either the player who failed to catch the ball or, more usually, the one who threw it becomes the Piggy. To make the game easier for the player in the middle, the rules can be modified so that Piggy only has to touch the ball rather than catch it. This can save shorter, butterfingered Piggies from humiliatingly long periods in the middle.

Piggy in the Middle can be played in larger groups, sometimes with the aid of a circle chalked on the ground. The players throwing the ball to each other must stay outside the circle at all times, while the Piggy must remain within it. This version can become fast and furious,

particularly in the version where the ball can only be held for a maximum of five seconds after being caught before it must be thrown again. Introducing more than one ball at a time enlivens the game even more, leading to a chaotic scene of body blows and dropped catches.

Taller players have an unfair advantage in Piggy in the Middle, as they can lob the ball high over other players' heads and more easily reach balls thrown between smaller players. One variation on the rules reduces this advantage by requiring players to bounce the ball at least once in the middle before it is caught.

Piggy in the Middle is also excellent fun when played in a swimming pool. All the players leaping right out of the water like salmon results in a great deal of splashing and white water.

How long children have been playing Piggy in the Middle is a matter for conjecture but the game is probably centuries old. The Romans played a game called *trigon* which is thought to have been similar. It involved three players, known as *trigonali*, who stood in a triangle and passed a hard ball backwards and forwards between them, catching the ball with the right hand and throwing it with the left. The *trigonali* had assistants called *pilecripi*, who did the scoring and chased after stray balls.

Piggy in the Middle is the usual name for the game in Britain but in the USA, where it is also widely played, it is most commonly known as 'Keep Away'. Other names used in the USA and Canada include 'Monkey in the Middle', 'Bear in the Middle', 'Monkey Snatches Ball' and even 'Pickle in a Dish'.

Pin the Tail on the Donkey

No Peeping Now

Tailless donkeys have long been a feature of children's parties. Why these beasts in particular should be singled out for anatomical experiment by small people is unclear. Whatever its origins, however, Pin the Tail on the Donkey remains a fixture of good parties, along with other confirmed favourites such as Pass the Parcel and Musical Chairs.

A drawing of a donkey minus its tail should be pinned to a wall or easel. The less artistically inclined should not be deterred; wonky donkeys are perfectly acceptable. The missing tail should be cut out from a piece of card and have a drawing pin or a piece of tape attached to it.

Each player in turn is blindfolded, with care being taken to make sure they cannot see. They are spun round a couple of times to disorient them (but not enough to make them too dizzy) and then positioned in front of the donkey and given the tail. They pin the tail onto the drawing at a spot they gropingly guess to be the donkey's hindquarters. The place each player chooses is marked by writing their name on the drawing. When everyone has had a turn, the player whose tail is closest to the correct position is declared the winner and receives a prize.

Although donkeys are the traditional subjects, there is no reason why another animal could not be substituted – pin the ear on the cat, perhaps, or the tongue on the dog. Or the animal theme could be abandoned for pinning the nose on the clown, the eye-patch on the pirate or the tiara on the princess. At Hallow'een, pinning the wart on the witch would be highly appropriate.

In Japan, children enjoy a similar game called *fukuwarai* ('lucky laugh'). Traditionally played at New Year, the game starts with a blank face and onto this the players pin various facial features, including eyes, eyebrows, nose and mouth. At the end, everyone stands back and enjoys the result.

On occasions, Pin the Tail on the Donkey has been used for a more serious purpose as an exercise for senior business managers. The participants are never told how close they came to getting the tails in the right place, demonstrating to them how lack of performance feedback can frustrate staff and hinder future progress.

Please Mr Crocodile

Snap Happy

Please Mr Crocodile is a chasing game with an enduring popularity. A piece of ground is designated as the river, and a player selected to be the Crocodile. The other players stand on one side of the river and call out 'Please, Mr Crocodile, may we cross your golden river?'. The Crocodile chooses a colour and tells the players that they may cross safely if they are wearing an item of clothing of that colour. Then all the players cross to the other side of the river; the players wearing the specified colour are able to stroll across, while those not wearing the colour have to rush over, trying to avoid being caught by the Crocodile.

Players who fall prey to the Crocodile are either declared out of the game or join the Crocodile in catching new victims. The process is repeated with a new colour and the players rush across the river in the other direction. The last player to remain uncaught becomes the Crocodile in the next round.

If played at school, a canny Crocodile will avoid selecting colours that are used in the uniform. The Crocodile cannot, of course, see what colour of underwear the players have on, but not every player is happy to show their knickers in order to prove immunity. Some keen players of the game have been known to carry a number of differently coloured hankies to stave off attack; and happy is the child whose mother has knitted or bought them a rainbow jumper!

As a change from colours, Crocodiles can grant immunity on various other grounds: to those with a certain letter in their name, or with a birthday in a certain month, or who had a particular cereal for breakfast, for instance.

Please Mr Crocodile

Although the rules are essentially the same, there are many regional names for this game. These include 'Boatman, Boatman', 'Farmer, Farmer, May We Cross Your Golden River?' and 'May I Cross the River?'. The versions of the plea to cross the river are highly inventive:

Please, Mr Porter,
May we cross your water
To see your ugly daughter
Swimming in the water?

Farmer, Farmer,
May we cross your golden river
In our silver boat?

Please, Jack, may I cross the water
To see the Queen's daughter?
My mother's gone, my father's gone,
And I want to go too.

Little is known about the origins of Please Mr Crocodile. It may be rather fanciful to see a parallel in Greek mythology with the final journey that the souls of the dead made across the River Styx to the underworld; but there is a similarity in the way that certain conditions had to be met (ie being dead, and paying the ferryman) before Charon the ferryman would consent to row people safely across the river.

Poohsticks
Stick, Stick, Stick!

People have probably always chucked sticks into rivers from bridges and then rushed across to the other side to see which one comes out first. But since the publication of the much-loved children's book *The House at Pooh Corner* by A A Milne in 1928, this charming pastime has had an official name: Poohsticks.

In chapter six, entitled 'In which Pooh invents a new game and Eeyore joins in', Winnie-the-Pooh accidentally drops not a stick but a fir cone into the river, and discovers that it slips quickly under the bridge and out the other side. He repeats this with two fir cones and tries to guess which will come out first, and then plays similar guessing games with different-sized fir cones. By the time he goes home for tea, he has predicted the winning fir cone 36 times and got it wrong 28 times.

Poohsticks is beautifully simple. Find a bridge and a reasonably fast-flowing stream or river. Forage for a stick for each player, or more than one if you want to have several rounds. Work out how to identify which stick belongs to which player; it helps if everyone selects sticks of different sizes and thicknesses. Then everyone stands on the bridge facing upstream with their stick-holding hand over the side of the bridge. Someone shouts 'Ready, steady, go', and on the word 'go', each player drops their stick into the water (throwing is not allowed). The players immediately rush across the bridge to the downstream side to see which stick comes out first from under the bridge. The winner is the owner of the first stick to emerge.

The bridge on which A A Milne and his son Christopher first played the game is in Ashdown Forest, close to the village of Hartfield in East Sussex. The World Poohsticks Championships take place on the River Thames each year at Day's Lock, near Dorchester-on-Thames in Oxfordshire. According to a member of the 2004 winning team from the Czech Republic, the secret is to spot the place where the river runs fastest and drop your stick there.

At the end of the Poohsticks episode in *The House at Pooh Corner*, Eeyore (who earlier has been found floating Poohstick-style down the river after being bounced into the water by Tigger) offers his own advice on Poohsticks technique; you should drop your stick in a 'twitchy sort of way', apparently. Wonder if it works?

Poor Puss!
Giggles Guaranteed

Poor Puss!, or 'Poor Pussy' as it is also known, is an old party favourite that is perfect for breaking the ice between guests who are shy or unacquainted, for it is certain to get them chuckling.

One player is chosen to be the Puss. The others sit round in a circle. Puss crawls round the circle on her hands and knees, picks on one of the players and sits in front of them miaowing and begging for attention. The chosen player strokes Puss on the head and says 'Poor Puss' three times, trying to keep a straight face while they do so.

Puss is allowed to do everything possible to get the other player to smile or laugh: make strange purring noises, pull faces, perform silly antics and so on. In some versions Puss is allowed to touch or tickle the other player. The other players in the circle are allowed to laugh, whistle, emit catcalls and do whatever they can to make it more difficult to keep that poker face. If a player's best efforts at muscle control fail and their face does break into a smile or they start to giggle, they become the next Puss.

The game can be turned on its head, with Puss remaining in the middle of the circle and the other players taking it in turns to crawl up to Puss and try to make her laugh. Whichever player is successful takes a turn as Puss. In a noisier version, each player whose resolution, and face, cracks must join the original Puss inside the circle and become a cat as well. This results in a whole clutter of cats in the middle, besieging the few players in the circle who have not yet succumbed to their wiles.

A more provocative version known as 'Darling, I Love You' has the player in the middle say to their victim 'Darling,

I love you, won't you give me a smile?'. The player so addressed then attempts to give straight-faced the reply 'Darling, I love you, but I just can't smile'. Common tactics for eliciting a laugh include sitting on the lap of the person who is the object of attention or kissing them on the cheek. This version is particularly suited to teenage parties where much of the fun of the game is causing the maximum embarrassment.

PLAYING OUT
Street Games of the 1950s

The 1950s was perhaps the last decade in which children's play was neither organized nor supervised. As yet streets were relatively empty of motor vehicles, and the civic creation of recreation grounds and play areas was in its infancy.

The bomb damage wreaked on many towns and cities during World War II was often still uncleared, providing children with ready-made and thrilling play areas, if perhaps not especially safe ones. 'In my neighbourhood, the sites of Hitler's bombs are many, and the bigger sites with a certain amount of rubble provide very good grounds for Hide and Seek and Tin Can Tommy', says a Peckham child of the 1950s, quoted in Iona and Peter Opie's *Children's Games in Street and Playground*.

According to some, the 1950s were a golden age in the long history of outdoor play. Writing in 1969, the Opies pulled no punches in lamenting the transformation of so many patches of waste ground and unmaintained grassy areas into municipal parks and play areas:

Having cleared away the places that are naturally wild it is becoming the fashion to set aside other places, deposit junk in them, and create 'Adventure Playgrounds', so called, the equivalent of creating Whipsnades for wildlife instead of erecting actual cages.

Iona and Peter Opie

In a typical 1950s street or playground, children might be observed playing Hopscotch, Marbles, Jacks, ball games against the wall, football with jumpers for goals, cricket with the wicket chalked on a wall, Cigarette-card Skimming, Spillikins (perhaps using wooden lolly sticks), skipping games (often using a washing line for the rope), clapping games, Tag, Grandmother's Footsteps, Cowboys and Indians or, just as likely, war games (Germans and English). The more audacious might venture a game of Knock Down Ginger or Truth or Dare.

Port and Starboard
Fun Ahoy!

This game is a nicely nautical diversion for landlubbers, possibly inspired by this island nation's seafaring past. It is an active game best played in a large room or outside, and requires only a leader and some participants ready, willing and able to obey their commands.

> **Bow!**
> *players run to the front wall*

> **Port!**
> *players run to the left side of the room*

When the leader calls a command, the other players perform the appropriate action. The last player to react is out. The winner is the last player left in the game.

The commands may be used in any sequence.

A great favourite with some Brownie packs was the command 'Up a Gum Tree'. When this command is issued, one player has to leap onto another's back, piggyback-style.

> **Starboard!**
> *players run to the right side of the room*

The faster the commands are barked out, the more uproarious the game becomes. And by the time it ends, every jolly Jack Tar in the room will surely know his port from his starboard.

> **Stern!**
> *players run to the back wall*

Davy Jones' Locker!
players find something to
stand on so that their feet are
no longer touching the floor

Boom Coming Over!
players duck down

Submarine!
players lie on their backs
with one leg in the air like
a periscope

Man Overboard!
players pretend to drown
('glug, glug, glug')

Hit the Deck!
players lie flat on their
stomachs

Scrub the Decks!
players drop to their hands and
knees and pretend to scrub
the floor

Climb the Rigging!
players pretend to
climb rigging

Mutiny!
players get into pairs and
pretend to swordfight

Captain's Coming!
players stand to
attention and salute

Man the Lifeboats!
players get into pairs, sit
down and row as if
in a boat

Seasick!
players mime being
sick (sound effects are
permitted)

Captain's Wife!
players curtsey

Stormy Weather!
players sway from side
to side

Postman's Knock
Special Delivery

Postman's Knock used to be a very popular party game, mainly for children of around four to seven years. Everyone sits on the floor in a circle. One person is chosen to play the Postman and goes out of the room, and another stands by the closed door. The Postman knocks on the door and when the door is opened the Postman says, 'Six letters for Janet' or 'Two letters for John', depending on which of the children in the room they want to summon and the number of letters they care to name. The named child goes out of the room to receive the same number of kisses as the number of letters specified. Once they have been given their 'letters', the kissed child remains outside the room to take their turn playing the part of the Postman.

To add an element of surprise to what could become a predictable game, each child in the room can be given a number. The Postman calls out a number instead of a name, and faces the consequences when the owner of that number comes forward!

In another version, all the boys gather in a group and each takes a card with a sequential number on it. The girls do the same. Then the boys stand in a line facing the girls, who are similarly lined up; each line should take care not to be in number order. One girl calls out a number and the boy with that number goes across and kisses her. Then a boy calls out a number and the selected girl goes and kisses him.

Spicier versions of Postman's Knock are reputed to be played at certain adult parties, with kisses not the only exchange required by way of a postal surcharge. But the most inventive variations on the game are probably those devised by the panellists of BBC Radio 4's *I'm Sorry I Haven't a Clue*. They came up with such memorable suggestions as 'Dustman's Knock' ('like Postman's Knock only filthier') and 'Surgeon's Knock' ('you go outside with a girl and stay there until she says "Cut it out"'). In its original form, however, Postman's Knock – like Kiss Chase – provides young children with a little innocent fun.

Queenie
Right Royal Fun

Queenie is a combination of guessing game and ball game, and used to be a particular favourite among girls.

One player is chosen to be Queenie and given the ball. Standing with her back to the other players, and without looking behind her, she throws the ball up over her head towards them, whereupon there is a scramble to be the first to catch it. Once the ball is caught, all the players stand with their hands behind their backs so that Queenie cannot tell which of them has the ball. Then they say:

Queenie, Queenie,
Who has the ball?
I haven't got it,
It isn't in my pocket.
Queenie, Queenie,
Who has the ball?

Or in another version:

Queenie, Queenie,
Who's got the ball?
Are they short or are they tall?
Are they hairy or are they bald?
You don't know because you don't have the ball.

Then Queenie turns round and says the name of the player she thinks has the ball. If she guesses correctly, she remains Queenie for another round. If her guess is wrong, the player who has successfully concealed the ball becomes Queenie.

Queenie does not have to make her guess straight away. She can ask various players to stretch out their hands or legs or twirl round in an attempt to find out who has the ball. The other players can try to confuse her by pretending to have the ball when they have not.

Sometimes Queenie is allowed more than one guess and so may be able to find out who has the ball by a process of elimination. However, if Queenie eliminates all the players but one, that player becomes Queenie.

Which queen gave her title to the game of Queenie, and why, is not known. And although two of the game's alternative names – 'Queen Anne' and 'Queen Mab' – are more specific about the sovereign in question, the reason for the naming remains obscure.

Ring a Ring of Roses

A Killing Game

Ring a ring of roses,
A pocket full of posies.
Atishoo, atishoo,
We all fall down!

This singing game is familiar to even the youngest children. Players join hands and walk or skip round in a circle while singing the famous song. On the word, 'down', everyone sits or falls quickly to the floor.

It is the song's history that makes Ring a Ring of Roses such an intriguing game. Generations of children have grown up with the notion that the words of the song refer to the plague, either the Great Plague of London in 1665 or the Black Death, which ravaged the population of Europe in the 14th century.

The 'ring of roses' is supposed to refer to the ring of red spots that were a symptom of bubonic plague, and the 'pocketful of posies' to the sweet-smelling flowers that people carried in the vain hope of warding off illness; as late as the 19th century it was widely believed that bad smells, rather than germs, caused diseases. Sneezing was another symptom, and as for the falling down – those who caught the plague were unlikely ever to get up again.

The version most often sung in the USA goes:

Ring around the rosie,
A pocketful of posies.
Ashes, ashes.
We all fall down!

Ring a Ring of Roses

Those of a macabre disposition might read into the word 'ashes' a reference to the burning of the bodies of plague victims. A simpler explanation might be that 'ashes' is a corruption of 'atishoo'.

However, the plague theory of the song's origin has fallen out of favour in recent years. Sceptics believe the song is more likely to date from the time of the Puritans, when dancing was banned. In those days, youngsters found one way to flout the ban was by playing games that were dances in disguise.

The debate about the origin of Ring a Ring of Roses rages on, rather like an outbreak of the dreaded illness it is supposed to describe. Offputting though a children's game might be that is packed with references to death and disease, there are versions of the song that include subsequent, lesser-known verses in which all the participants jump up again, alive and well enough to dance another day. These include:

The King has sent his daughter,
To fetch a pail of water.
Atishoo, atishoo.
We all fall down!

The bird up on the steeple
Sits high above the people.
Atishoo, atishoo.
We all fall down!

The cows are in the meadow
Eating buttercups.
Atishoo, atishoo.
They all jump up!

Fishes in the water,
Fishes in the sea,
We all jump up,
With a one, two, three!

Sitting at the bottom of the deep blue sea,
Catching fishes for my tea.
We all jump up,
With a one, two, three!

SIGN HERE
The Craze for Autograph Books

For most children, opportunities to meet famous people are rare. Despite this, many girls from the early 20th century onwards owned an autograph book that they would fill, not with the signatures of celebrities of the day but with verses and drawings penned by friends and classmates. It was traditional to collect autographs at the end of the school year, particularly if one was leaving or moving to another school.

There were lots of rhymes to accompany the signatures, many of which relied on code (surprisingly similar to today's textspeak), innuendo and a liberal sprinkling of exclamation marks. Most were mildly insulting; a few were mawkishly sentimental. And in later life, autograph book verses are wonderfully nostalgic, even if memories of the people who penned them have long since faded.

2 Ys U R
2 Ys U B
I C U R
2 Ys 4 Me

If all the boys lived over the sea what a good swimmer [name of recipient] would be!!

When I die, do not cry, I'll send you all my riches
A garden fork, a cabbage stalk and a pair of mouldy britches!

Little Birdie flying high
Dropping presents from the sky
Angry Farmer wiping eye
Thank the Lord that cows can't fly!!!

1 1 was a racehorse
2 2 was 1 2
1 1 1 1 race
2 2 1 1 2

We all sat on the green green grass
The greenest we could find
But [name] sat on something that
The cows had left behind!!!

Don't make love at the garden gate,
Love may be blind, but the neighbours ain't!!!

My heart is like a cabbage
Divided into two.
The leaves I give to anyone,
My heart I give to you …

Two in a hammock
Attempted to kiss
And in less than a trice
They finished like this

198

Her eyes she got from her father
Her nose from her mother meek
But where in all creation
Did she get her blessed cheek?

I only ask this little spot
In which to write Forget me not.

When you are married and have twins,
Don't come to me for safety pins.

The tall pink foxglove bowed his head.

The violets curtsied and went to bed

Monica.
July 1924

And on the last page:

By hook or by crook, I'll be last in your book.

although if space permitted, someone else might squeeze in:

By water and fire, I'll prove you a liar.

Rounders

A Sport for All

A game of rounders and a sunny afternoon in the park go together like, well, bat and ball. After everyone has eaten far too many picnic goodies at lunchtime, some post-prandial exercise is called for. Everyone is cajoled into a game of rounders. Even Granny, and Great Uncle John with his dodgy knee, and cousin Julia who is wearing a most unsuitable floaty frock.

All that is needed for rounders is a bat (a baseball bat is perfect, but a cricket bat will do) and a relatively soft ball, like a tennis ball. Four 'bases' – first, second, third and fourth – are marked out in the corners of the playing pitch with jumpers, coats or whatever else is to hand.

Two teams are selected, and a coin is tossed to see which will bat first. The fielding team positions one player on or close to each base and a backstop behind the batter (like a wicketkeeper in cricket) with one player bowling. Any other players on this team disperse themselves around the field.

The first batter proceeds to the batting position, which is roughly in the middle of the playing pitch. The bowler bowls underarm, aiming the ball at above knee height, and the batter tries to whack the ball as far away as possible. Then they make a run to first base, and to the bases beyond if they have time before the ball is retrieved, although a batter that hits the ball behind themself can only run as far as first base. Batters must run round the outside of each base; taking a short cut to glory by running inside the bases is strictly forbidden.

While the batter is running, the fielders try to touch a base with the ball before the batter reaches it; if this happens, the batter is out. Batters can also be caught out, as in

cricket. Once the bowler has the ball back in his hands, no running is allowed.

When the next batter steps up to the batting area and another ball is bowled, any batter at one of the bases can make a run in an attempt to get round the rest of the bases. As it is against the rules to have more than one batter at any base, batters have to be careful not to run out their teammates.

If a batter reaches fourth base in one turn, they have made a rounder, and their team gets a point. If a batter takes more than one turn to reach fourth base, they make half a rounder. Batters who have completed a circuit return to the batting line to wait for their next turn. Once all the batting side is out, the fielding side takes a turn at batting. The winning team is the one that scores the most rounders.

Strictly speaking, the rule is that batters have to run whether they hit the ball or not, but in more informal games this rule might be waived, allowing players three chances to hit the ball before they have to run. The exception to this is when a no-ball is bowled, ie one that is overarm, overhead, below the knee, bounces or goes too wide for the batter to reach. If there are three no-balls in succession, the batting team is awarded half a rounder penalty. Of course, if the batter wishes to hit a no-ball, they can try!

Having been played since Tudor times, Rounders can claim to be the precursor of sports such as baseball and softball, which became formalized and commercialized. The whole point about Rounders, however – and the reason it is such great fun – is that it need never be taken too seriously. It is a supremely egalitarian pursuit open to all-comers: short, fat, fit, unfit, old, young, those who cannot throw for toffee, and those who really could not hit a ball to save their life. None of these things matter when the grass is green and the sun is shining.

Simon Says

Or Does He?

This is a simple game to play with young children, and also teaches that vital skill: listening carefully.

Someone (often an adult) plays the part of Simon. All the other players stand facing them, making sure they have a bit of space around them.

Simon issues a series of instructions, preceded by the words 'Simon says'. For example:

Simon says: Touch your toes.

Simon says: Put your hands on your head.

Simon says: Turn around.

At some point, however, Simon will say merely 'Clap your hands' or 'Fold your arms' without prefacing the order with 'Simon says'. Any player who performs the action when it is not preceded by this phrase is out. The last player to be eliminated wins. As the game progresses, Simon can redouble his efforts to catch out savvier players of the game by barking out a number of orders very quickly, one after the other, but one of them will not be a Simon Says.

Simon says lift your right leg!

Amusing though it may be, Simon must resist the temptation to issue impossible commands such as 'Simon says lift your right leg. Simon says lift your left leg. Ha, Simon did not say put your right leg down'.

The game of Simon Says is found in many countries. In France it is known as *Jacques a dit* ('James says'), in the

Netherlands as *Commando* ('I command') and in Norway as *Kongen befaler,* meaning 'the king commands'.

Psychological studies have found that as well as teaching listening skills, the game is a good way of helping children to improve their self-control and to rein in impulsive behaviour. In the end, though, how well someone does in a game of Simon Says probably comes down to how comfortable they are with obeying orders. Those of a more rebellious nature might find the game hard to tolerate for long.

Skipping Games
Rope Tricks

For decades, girls everywhere have spent hours of their lives engaged in skipping games. As gym bunnies and boxers know, skipping is fantastic exercise, and skipping games can be played either solo by one girl turning the rope for herself, or by three or more players, with two turning a longer rope for the others to jump over. In multi-player games, skippers must exercise great skill in timing a run at the already turning rope, so that they start their turn with a neat jump, rather than a tangle of rope and ankles and a humiliating fall to the ground.

Inevitably, however, there will come a point when, owing to lack of skill or the tired dragging of feet, the skipping player will make a mistake, whereupon they should be replaced by one of the players turning the rope.

There are a myriad skipping rhymes to recite while jumping. Some incorporate actions that allow accomplished skippers to show off their skills. Here is just a small selection:

I am a Girl Guide dressed in blue,
These are the actions I can do,
Stand at attention, stand at ease,
Bend my elbows, bend my knees.
Salute to the officers,
Bow to the Queen,
Show my knickers to the
football team
[the player flashes her knickers, or pretends to!]

Teddy bear, teddy bear, turn around
Teddy bear, teddy bear, touch the ground
Teddy bear, teddy bear, show your shoe
[player lifts foot in the air]
Teddy bear, teddy bear, that will do!
[waggles finger side to side]
Teddy bear, teddy bear, go upstairs
[mimes taking steps]
Teddy bear, teddy bear, say your prayers
[clasps hands together]
Teddy bear, teddy bear, turn out the light
[mimes turning off a switch]
Teddy bear, teddy bear, say goodnight
[player runs out]

I'm a little bumper [or bubble] car, number 48,
I whizzed round the corner
[player must leave rope, run round the back of one
of the players holding it and run back in again, all
the while prolonging the pronunciation of the word
'cornerrrrrrrrrrrrrrrr']

And slammed on my brakes.
Policeman came and put me in jail.
How many days did he put me in jail?
1, 2, 3, 4, 5, 6 ...
[counting continues until the skipping player makes a mistake, then the next player tries to beat their score]

Apples, pears, peaches, plums,
Tell me when your birthday comes.
January, February, March, April ...
[the skipping player lists the months until their own birthday month; on reaching it they run out]

Sometimes more than one skipper jumps the rope at the same time, running in to jump in sequence or when their name is called. Things can get quite crowded!

I love coffee, I love tea.
I want [name of person] *in with me.*
[the named player joins the skipper]
I hate coffee, I hate tea.
I hate [named person] *in with me.*
[their erstwhile companion runs out again]

I had a little puppy,
His name was Tiny Tim.
I put him in the bathtub to see if he could swim.
He drank all the water, he ate a bar of soap,
The next thing I know he had a bubble in his throat.
In came the doctor [the next player runs in]
In came the nurse [a second player runs in]
In came the lady with the alligator purse
[a third player runs in]
Out went the doctor [the first player runs out]

Out went the nurse [the second player runs out]
Out went the lady with the alligator purse
[the third player runs out]

All in together, girls,
Never mind the weather, girls.
When I call your birthday, you must jump in.
January, February, March ...
[the other players jump in when their birthday month is mentioned]

One of the simplest skipping rhymes – 'Salt, vinegar, mustard, pepper' – is far from simple to perform. Either the rope is turned faster and faster as the rhyme is repeated, or the rope is turned at double speed on the word 'pepper' and the player must clear the rope twice with one jump. A spicy challenge indeed!

Sleeping Lions

The Hunters and the Hunted

This popular party game for young children has the added benefit for adults of bringing a few welcome moments of stillness and quiet to the proceedings.

All the children lie on the floor as still as they can, with their eyes closed in the guise of Sleeping Lions. Either one or two children can be chosen to be the Hunters, or an adult can assume the role.

The Hunters walk around the room and attempt to get the Lions to move by talking to them and trying to make them laugh, but not by touching them. Any Lion who moves is either out of the game or gets up and joins the Hunters. The last Sleeping Lion left in the game is the winner.

The game of Sleeping Lions has a host of alternative names, including 'Dead Soldiers' (rather macabre), 'Standing Scarecrows' (the players have to stand still rather than lie down), 'Resting Tigers' and 'Sleeping Logs' (though whoever saw a log wake up?).

Given the pandemonium that prevails at children's parties, adults might find themselves enjoying the peace and quiet so much that they decide to let Sleeping Lions lie!

Spillikins

Pick Up Sticks

Spillikins is a game of skill and sleight of hand played with a bundle of around 40 thin pointed sticks. Nowadays the sticks are usually made of plastic, but in the past they were made of wood, bone or even ivory, and were sometimes beautifully carved or realized in different types of wood.

Spillikins often come in varying colours to represent the different scores they award to the player who captures them. Other sets award scores according to different shapes; a popular white plastic set of the 1970s was shaped like miniature garden tools, with spades, hoes, forks and saws.

To start the game a player holds all the sticks in a bunch in their hand so that they poke out of their fist as it rests on the ground or the table. The player lets the sticks go so that they fan out and fall into a pile in a 'spill'.

Players then take turns to try to remove one stick from the pile without moving any of the other sticks. As players ease their stick gingerly out of the pile, their every move will be closely policed by the other players. If there is any movement among the other sticks, the player is out and the next player takes a turn. However, if a player succeeds in picking up a stick without causing any disturbance, they add it to their hoard and score however many points are awarded for that stick's colour or shape. A successful capture also wins another turn. The winner is the player with the most sticks, or the highest score, once all the sticks have been retrieved.

Various techniques can be used to pick up a stick. If a stick is lying on top of the others, a player can:

- push down on one end to raise the other end off the pile so that it can be grasped.

- press down gently and slowly draw the stick backwards off the pile.

- pluck one off with finger and thumb.

Some favour removing the sticks at speed, which makes it harder to detect movement of the other sticks. Others adopt a more cautious approach, weighing up their options for several minutes before going in for the steal.

In most Spillikin sets, there are a handful of special sticks; these may be pointed at both ends instead of only one, or a particular shape or colour, or hooked at one end. If a player manages to snaffle one of these coveted sticks they do not score any points but can use this stick to help them flick or hook other sticks off the pile, a concession which, used properly and not too recklessly, can pave the way to a quick victory.

Spillikins also goes by the names of 'Spellicans', 'Pick Up Sticks', 'Mikado' and 'Jack Straws'. Similar stick games are thought to have been played in India at the time of the Buddha, and also in ancient China, where the throwing of sticks was a method of divination. Native Americans are thought to have played the game with wheat straws.

So players of Spillikins are following in a long tradition. They are also in illustrious company; Jane Austen was a fan of the game, as she makes clear in a letter of 1807 that describes the visit of a young guest: 'Half her time here was spent at Spillikins; which I consider as a very valuable part of our household furniture'.

Stone, Paper, Scissors

Not a Game of Chance

O h, the beautiful simplicity of a game that can be played with nothing but one's bare hands!

Two players each put one of their hands behind their backs and count to three. On 'three' they bring the hand out in front of them again, making the form of a stone (the hand shaped into a fist), a piece of paper (the palm held out flat) or a pair of scissors (two fingers held apart like scissor blades).

Stone beats Scissors, because it can blunt them; the winner taps their opponent's Scissors with their Stone to symbolize this.

Paper beats Stone, because it can be wrapped around it; the winner wraps their Paper around their opponent's Stone.

Scissors beat Paper, because they can cut it; the winner pretends to cut their opponent's Paper with their Scissors.

The winner of Stone, Paper, Scissors is often decided on a 'best of three rounds' basis. If both players make the same 'throw', it is a draw and they start again.

Versions of Stone, Paper, Scissors have existed for centuries. A tomb that dates from 2000 BC at Beni Hassan, Egypt, includes among its paintings a scene believed to depict a similar 'finger-flashing' game. Today the game exists in various forms in cultures around the world.

The game is usually known as 'Rock, Paper, Scissors' (or RPS) in the USA. In Japan, *Jan Ken Pon* or *Poi* is a slightly more sophisticated and centuries-old version that is still widely played. Another name for the game in some parts of France and the USA is *Rochambeau* or *Roshambo*, in honour of the Count of Rochambeau, a French hero of the American War of Independence who is supposed to have triumphed in a game of Stone, Paper, Scissors over no less an opponent than George Washington. In Indonesia, the game is known as 'Earwig, Elephant, Man'; the Elephant crushes the Man, the Man crushes the Earwig, and the Earwig beats the Elephant by climbing into its ear and driving it insane.

Expert adult players of Stone, Paper, Scissors – including those who regularly participate in the world championship organized by the World RPS Society   insist that it is a game of strategy rather than a game of chance. A number

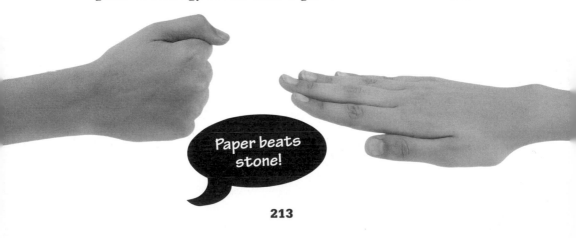

Paper beats stone!

of three-throw gambits have been formulated that are said to give a player more chance of winning by exploiting the non-random behaviour of their opponent. For example, men apparently lead most often with Stone, while women favour Scissors.

Children often use Stone, Paper, Scissors as a way of deciding matters such as who goes first in a game – the equivalent of tossing a coin. Amazingly, the game has also been used in a similar way by adults, but to settle much more serious disputes when more conventional methods of arbitration have failed.

In one notable case recently, a Japanese corporation that wished to sell its valuable collection of Impressionist paintings could not decide whether to have them auctioned by Christie's or Sotheby's. In the end, the contract was awarded in accordance with the outcome of a game of Stone, Paper, Scissors; Christie's Scissors beat Sotheby's Paper.

Scissors beat paper!

Stone Skimming

Shore to Please

The pleasure of whiling away an hour or so on the banks of a pond or lake by skimming stones across the water should not be underestimated. If you have the knack, that is! Otherwise the feeling is more likely to be one of frustration as skimming attempts result in nothing more dramatic than a resounding single plop as the stone plummets to the bottom. But with the right stones and a honed technique, you will be skimming stones with the best of them.

The secret lies in choosing a flat stone, and an expedition in search of suitably shaped ones is part and parcel of any serious stone-skimming session. Then skimmers must perfect a sideways flick of the wrist to give the stone the required trajectory so that it hits the water at speed and at the flattest possible angle. Adopting a low stance helps, as does that all-important flick, to give the stone the required horizontal spin. A skimmer who manages seven or eight bounces is doing very well.

Stone Skimming is known to some as 'Ducks and Drakes', perhaps because the ripple effect produced resembles the patterns made by a dipping waterfowl. The old expression 'to play ducks and drakes' with something means to fritter away or squander something of value, like someone throwing stones into a river carelessly, for the sake of amusement. In centuries past, people are thought to have skimmed flat shells such as oyster shells as well as stones.

A keen observer might notice that males, who seem to be genetically programmed to throw stones into water from an early age, are more likely to practise Stone Skimming. Father–son bonding regularly takes place over skimming sessions, with senior males keen to pass on their secret techniques to a younger generation of skimmers. The engineer and inventor Sir Barnes Wallis, of Dambusters fame, supposedly conceived the idea of a 'bouncing' bomb while skimming stones with his children. Females are often keen to have a go at Stone Skimming too, but can be discouraged by that cruel adage 'girls can't throw'.

Yet even the most accomplished stone skimmer could spend a lifetime trying and failing to better the record of Russ Byers, an American who holds the world record for 'Stone Skipping' (as skimming is known in the USA). In 2007, he managed to skim a stone so that it touched the surface of a river in Pennsylvania an astonishing 51 times before finally sinking into the depths; the previous record was a mere 40.

Tag
The Thrill of the Chase

If there was a prize for the most popular playground game of all, Tag would take the honours every time. Almost universal, endlessly versatile, unfailingly rousing, Tag allows children to do what they like best: run around.

In the basic game of Tag (or 'Tig', 'It', 'Touch', 'Catch', 'Dobby', 'He' or 'Tick' as it is also known) one player is chosen to be It or On or, in some places, He. Off they go in pursuit of the other players in the game until they succeed in catching up with someone, touching them and triumphantly calling out 'Tag' (or 'Tig'). The tagged player then becomes It. Immediately tagging back the person who tagged you ('double-touching') is not normally allowed.

Taunting of the player who is On – along the lines of 'Ha, ha, ha, hee, hee, hee, you can't catch me for a bumble bee' – is an essential part of the game.

Tag games go on and on until the bell rings for lessons. Or until players cannot run any more and have to flop down to catch their breath.

Such a simple game as Tag lends itself to an almost infinite number of variations. Here are just a few:

Stuck in the Mud
Anyone who has been tagged has to stand on the spot, either with their legs apart or with their arms held out, until another player releases them by crawling between their legs or ducking under one of their outstretched arms. It is common to have two or more players as It in this version because they remain in the role throughout the game. Stuck in the Mud is also known as 'Scarecrow Tag' or 'Frozen Tag', for obvious reasons.

Off-ground Tag

This version is played like ordinary Tag except that the player being chased can make themselves 'safe' by standing on a base, such as a brick or bench, the top of a dustbin or astride a fence, etc. They cannot be tagged as long as their whole body is off the ground. It is considered bad form, however, to spend too much time 'off ground'; such behaviour may provoke the taunt of 'Scaredy cat!' or 'Cowardy, cowardy custard!'.

Hopping He

Everyone must hop – both the pursuer and the pursued. Similarly, in 'Walking He' the players may only walk; and in 'Shadow He' a player is tagged by someone stepping on their shadow – which restricts this version to sunny days!

Chain Tag

In this version, when a player is tagged they join hands with It, and the two of them run round together trying to catch more people for the chain. Gradually the chain gets longer, more unwieldy and difficult for the other players to avoid as it swings wildly around like a great thrashing snake. 'Pairs He' is a less chaotic version in which two players join hands and chase the others. When a third person is tagged they join onto the original pair; when a fourth player is tagged, they split into two pairs, and so on.

Toilet Tag

This is a contemporary version which young children in particular find hilarious. A tagged player becomes a 'toilet' and has to squat down with a hand held out for the 'flusher'. They can be freed if another player comes along and 'flushes' their hand.

MANY HAPPY RETURNS
The 1970s Birthday Party

The children's birthday party of the 1970s was almost always held at home. A few weeks beforehand, a little cardboard invitation would be delivered to the prospective guests, usually with a tear-off slip at the bottom on which to write one's RSVP.

Some degree of dressing-up was still de rigueur: for girls, a home-made velvet party frock, and for boys, shorts, shirt and tie, and hair combed flat for once.

Once all the guests had arrived, the party games would begin in the balloon-bedecked lounge. A typical programme boasted a combination of the following:

Pass the Parcel – the layers always consisted of newspaper, and it was almost unheard of to insert prizes between the layers, although luxury versions might stretch to the occasional fruit pastille.

Musical Chairs/Statues/Bumps – this perennial favourite had everyone marching round, standing still or bumping down on a swirly-patterned, wall-to-wall fitted carpet in fashionable orange and brown hues.

Things on a Tray (Kim's Game) – the selection of objects would be carried in by Mum on one of her flowery melamine trays, covered with an equally flowery tea-towel that would be whipped off for two minutes while everyone tried to commit the items to memory.

Postman's Knock – this game was often deeply embarrassing for the children involved, unless they were still young enough not to mind kissing someone of the opposite sex. It usually gave parents a laugh, though.

Pin the Tail on the Donkey – another must, although in those pre-Blu-Tack® days a drawing pin was always used, leaving the lounge wall studded with holes.

After the party games, the party food! Draped with a scallop-edged paper cloth, the tea table would groan with edible delights. Plying paper plates and paper napkins, guests could help themselves to:

Sandwiches – always white bread with the crusts cut off, and filled with egg and cress, ham, cheese spread, meat paste or Marmite®. The different types would be labelled with a little flag stuck in one of the sandwiches.

Sausages on sticks – no party table was complete without these, and some children could get through a prodigious number.

Cheese cubes and tinned pineapple chunks on sticks – less popular than the sausages, but a fixture nevertheless. An alternative was a plate of those foil-wrapped little cheese triangles, still available today.

To drink – squash, invariably orange but occasionally blackcurrant-flavoured, served from big coloured plastic jugs into paper cups that went soggy and started to collapse after a few refills.

'Afters' was invariably jelly or blancmange, usually strawberry-flavoured and always served in little waxed paper dishes with frilled edges. Sometimes, Mum would have put slices of banana into the jelly before it set, a practice many children found revolting, but this was the only concession made to healthy eating.

The birthday cake was, almost without fail, pink for a girl and blue for a boy; the appropriate colouring was added to the glacé icing on a Victoria sponge cake sandwiched with strawberry jam. The name and age of the birthday child was usually piped onto the icing in white. Occasionally, a more creative mother would go to town with chocolate finger biscuits or desiccated coconut dyed green to create a fort or football field.

Once the candles were blown out and a wish made, left-over slices of cake were wrapped in paper napkins to be taken home by the guests. Party bags were a relatively recent innovation and were much less lavish than those of today. Children would go home deliriously happy with an elasticated plastic bracelet, a whistle or a yo-yo, along with the usual balloon and piece of cake.

Three-legged Race
A Bit Tied-Up

The three-legged race is common feature of school sports days, when pairs of tied-together children in gym shorts attempt to waddle their way along a course, arms wrapped tightly round one another, desperately trying not to humiliate themselves in front of their eagerly watching parents and classmates by falling over.

The usual method of binding children together is by means of a scarf. The left leg of one player is tied to the right leg of the other just above the ankle and the scarf tied tightly enough to prevent it coming undone under considerable strain, but not so tight as to stop the circulation.

The secret of success in a three-legged race is practice; players need to develop coordination with their partner beforehand so that they get into a rhythm: double-leg forward, outside legs forward, double-leg forward, and so on. With practice they should soon be moving like a well-oiled machine. But fail to get the sequence right and they will end up flat on their backs in an unseemly heap of arms and legs, or with a twisted ankle or two.

Three-legged races – often in fancy dress – are a common feature of charity events, when the opportunity to make a fool of yourself in a good cause is, for once, welcome.

The essential point about the three-legged race is that it requires a degree of harmony between partners in order to have a successful outcome. To this extent the race can be seen as a metaphor for a successful life partnership. Though moving forward may be difficult at times – you may come a cropper or sustain the odd knock – stick together through thick and thin and you will stay the course.

Tiddlywinks
Squidgy Stuff

Although sometimes seen as a childish pastime, Tiddlywinks is a sport requiring an amazing degree of skill and dexterity if it is to be played well. Its devotees consider it a game of tactics akin to chess.

The basic action in Tiddlywinks involves snapping the edge of a large flat disc (a 'squidger') quickly down onto the edge of a smaller flat disc (a 'wink') so that the wink flicks either into a receptacle – usually a cup – in the centre of the playing area, or on top of an opponent's wink. Over the years, winks have been made out of ivory, bone, celluloid, wood and even metal, but nowadays are invariably made of coloured plastic.

Each player uses six winks, two large and four small; different colours – normally red, blue, green and yellow – identify which winks belong to each player. The game is often played in pairs: red and blue always team up against green and yellow. Tiddlywink sets come with a felt mat of around six feet by three feet in size that marks out the playing area. The winks start in the corners, one for each colour, with the pot placed in the middle.

A 'squidge-off' decides who goes first. Everyone shoots one of the winks towards the pot. The person whose wink lands nearest starts.

Players then take it in turns to flick a wink, trying either to get it into the pot or to cover ('squop') an opponent's wink; the point of this is to stop other players getting within firing distance of the pot. Once a wink has been covered either fully or partially, it may not be played, although it can be rescued by firing other winks at the one on top. The wink on top can still be played, and some players become very skilled at flicking several winks off a pile, either one at a time or all in one go. Any player who successfully lands a wink in the pot gets another go.

The game ends when all the winks of one colour have been potted or after a specified length of time, when total points ('tiddlies') for each player are totted up according to the number of winks each has potted (three points each) or remain unsquopped (two points each).

Tiddlywinks has some colourful terms. Here is a selection:

- blitz – a player's attempt to pot all of their six winks early in the game.

- bomb – to fire a wink at a pile of winks in the hope of disturbing it.

- cracker – a shot that knocks one wink off the top of another while simultaneously squopping it.

- crud – a forceful shot aimed at destroying a pile of winks completely.

- scrunge – to bounce out of the pot.

- sub – to play a wink so that it ends up under another wink.

Originally known as Tiddledy Winks, Tiddlywinks was invented in Victorian times and became a huge craze in the 1890s with both adults and children. It underwent something of a revival at Cambridge University in the 1950s. Well, why study when you could be aiming a crud at someone's winks instead?

Tin Can Tommy
I Get a Kick Out of You

The sound of cans being kicked during a rousing game of Tin Can Tommy has resonated in streets from Inverness to Penzance since long before World War I, waking up sleeping babies and inducing headaches in adults within earshot. Part of the game's appeal in the more impoverished days of yesteryear was the lack of expense, empty tin cans being easy to beg or borrow and their shape, size and condition being immaterial.

The players select a base – a drain cover is ideal, or a circle chalked on the road – and choose a player to be the Canner, also known as the Guard or Denner.

The game starts with the Canner kicking the can as far as possible while the rest of the players run off and hide, usually within agreed boundaries. The Canner retrieves the can and returns to the base, shouting 'Tin-Off' as he places the can on the base before going off in search of the other players. As soon the Canner spots another player, he rushes back to put his foot on the can and shouts out 'Tin

Can Tommy, one, two, three' followed by the name of the person he has seen. That person has to come out of hiding and go to stand on the base. However, they can be freed at any time if a player still in the game manages to run to the base and kick away the can. In some versions, the person who has been spotted must race the Canner back to the can and try to kick it before the Canner can tag them.

There are many different rules and variations. For example, procuring the can is sometimes part of the game, with the last person to find a can having to take on the dreaded role of Canner. Sometimes the Canner has to walk backwards to the base with the can once he has retrieved it, and then walk round the base ten times, or count to 300 in fives before going off to search for the other players.

The role of Canner is not easy, and can be almost impossible if there are a lot of players. As the number of captives increases, the Canner, understandably, becomes more and more reluctant to leave them at the can for long. But he still has to make regular forays in search of the other players. A Canner who sticks to his can runs the risk of being taunted by his captives. In Scotland, one such chant goes:

> *Leave the den, ye dirty hen,*
> *An' look for a' yer chickens.*

The beauty of Tin Can Tommy is that it can be adapted easily to the surroundings in which it is being played, hence variants like 'Tag the Pole' or 'Tag the Tree'. The game is sometimes played with a football or even a bucket instead of a can. But most of its many regional names – 'Kick the Can', 'Tin Can Jerky', 'Tin Can Alley', 'Rin Tin Tin' and 'Tin the Block' – derive from the classic tin can version.

Tongue-twisters
What a Mouthful!

Tongue-twisters provide a vigorous and entertaining workout for the mouth. Most rely on excruciating alliteration and rhyme or the quick-fire repetition of diphthongs rarely so crowded together in normal spoken English. But the most entertaining aspect of tongue-twisters is that they contain arrant nonsense.

Tongue-twisters vary in length from just a couple of words repeated over and over again at increasing speed (try 'Peggy Babcock') to whole stanzas of contortion that only the very agile of mouth will succeed in reciting without error. For example:

You've no need to light a night-light
On a light night like tonight,
For a night-light's light's but a slight light,
And tonight's a night that's light.
When a night's light, like tonight's light,
It is really not quite right
To light night-lights with their slight lights
On a light night like tonight.

No-one knows for how long people have been tying themselves up in tongue-twisters – probably for as long as people have been picking pecks of pickled peppers. Examples from art and literature are numerous. In Shakespeare's *The Tempest*, Caliban is moved by Miranda's beauty to remark, 'But she as far surpasseth Sycorax, As great'st does least'. And who can forget Eliza Doolittle in *My Fair Lady* attempting to enunciate the immortal line 'In Hertford, Hereford and Hampshire, hurricanes hardly ever happen'? Gilbert and Sullivan, who produced such lyrics as 'He is the very model of a modern major general', were clearly tongue-twister fans, as was Dr Seuss, who penned 'Oscar's only ostrich oiled an orange owl today'.

Other firm favourites include:

She sells seashells on the seashore.

Round and round the rugged rock the ragged rascal ran.

Fuzzy Wuzzy was a bear. Fuzzy Wuzzy had no hair. Fuzzy Wuzzy wasn't fuzzy, was he?

Every language has its own tongue-twisters. Linguists might like to try the German *Zwischen zwei Zweigen zwitschern zwei Schwalben* ('two swallows twitter between two branches'), or this French example, the English translation of which is almost as difficult to say: *Si six scies scient six cyprès, six cent scies scient six-cent cyprès* ('if six saws saw six cypresses, six hundred saws saw six hundred cypresses').

The joy of tongue-twisters is that sooner or later everyone meets their Waterloo, however articulate they are. Here are some particularly challenging one-liners.

You know you need unique New York.

Greek grapes.

Red lorry, yellow lorry, red lorry, yellow lorry.

Chopstick shops sell chopsticks.

Many an anemone sees an enemy anemone.

If Stu chews shoes, should Stu choose the shoes he chews?

All I want is a proper cup of coffee, made in a proper copper coffee pot.

A bloke's back bike brake block broke.

The sixth sick sheikh's sixth sheep's sick.

Can you imagine an imaginary menagerie manager imagining managing an imaginary menagerie?

Which wristwatches are Swiss wristwatches?

Freshly fried fresh flesh.

Girl gargoyle, guy gargoyle.

A green glass gas globe.

Traffic Lights

Ready, Steady, Go

There are two versions of this far-from-pedestrian party game, one for younger and one for older children. The game can be played indoors or out, but plenty of space is needed for both versions.

The first is more suitable for very small children, particularly those with a penchant for cars, fire engines, lorries and all things vehicular. It is not the quietest of games, but it is a great way for excited partygoers to work off some of their energy.

A little advance preparation is needed. Take three pieces of white card – circular would be most appropriate but square is fine – and colour one green, one red and one orange (or as close a colour to amber as possible).

When the children are assembled, get them to choose what sort of vehicle they would like to be – car, lorry, bus, fire engine, ambulance, etc – and then ask them to 'drive' round the room, making the appropriate vrooming, beeping and siren noises. It might be wise to ask everyone to move in the same direction to avoid collisions!

At intervals, hold up one of the pieces of coloured card. If it is the red card, shout 'Stop, the lights are red', and the children must stand still. If orange, the call is 'Slow down, the lights are amber', and the children must slow right down, or perhaps run on the spot. If the card is green, shout 'Go, go, go, the lights are green' and the children can continue on their way. A few obstacles can be introduced, such as a roundabout (the children must run in a small circle), a traffic jam (the children must go extra slowly) or a speed bump (the children must give a little leap in the air before continuing). At the end of the game, the children have to find a parking space before they leave their vehicles.

In the version for older children, one of them plays the part of the Traffic Light. The Traffic Light stands at one end of the room with their back to everyone else. The rest of the children line up at the other end, facing the Traffic Light. The game starts when the Traffic Light shouts 'Green light!'. The other players then creep up behind them as fast as they can until the Traffic Light turns round suddenly, shouting 'Red light!'. On this command everyone must freeze instantly. The last person to stop moving is sent back to the start line. The game continues until someone succeeds in creeping up and tagging the Traffic Light without being seen. The successful player then takes on the role of the Traffic Light.

Truth or Dare
Is Honesty the Best Policy?

Truth or Dare is a game that produces a decided frisson. It is not so much the Dare part, although the tasks can be scary, as the chilling prospect of having to confess to one's innermost secrets and desires in the Truth category.

This is a game that can be played in any place and at any time, but the most memorable sessions of Truth or Dare usually take place in the evening; twilight and darkness seem to bring out a guilty but slightly delicious feeling of doing something one should not, ideal for a confessional game in which no one can be sure what will happen next.

One person begins the game by asking another player whether they will take a Truth or a Dare. If they choose a Truth, the other players devise a question for them, which should be answered truthfully. This is usually a personal question of the 'Do you fancy Chris?' variety.

If the player chooses a Dare, they are required to perform some kind of outrageous forfeit. This is often a prank such as knocking on doors and running away, or perhaps kissing someone who is considered particularly unattractive. Occasionally, dangerous dares are set, with illegal or tragic consequences. But happily, most games of Truth or Dare are harmless, if somewhat humiliating.

A more complex version of the game goes by the extended name of 'Truth, Dare, Promise or Opinion'. If a player opts for a Promise, they must make a promise to do something in the near future, such as buy chocolate for all the players. If they opt for an Opinion, they will be asked to give their honest opinion about something. This is almost always their opinion of one of the other players or someone who is not present, rather than on a burning political issue; other players are much more interested in who likes or hates who.

Truth or Dare tends to be played by older children, particularly those beginning to taste independence, and racier versions of the game are sometimes embarked upon late at night by adults, particularly if they are a little the worse for drink! But it is questionable how much truth is told when the Truth option is chosen. Players are honour-bound to tell the truth in theory, but in practice fibbing is probably widespread, although the edginess of the game can heighten sensibilities enough to make players as alert to untruths as a lie detector.

PLUS ÇA CHANGE ...
A Snapshot of Today's Playground

A cloudy but mild playtime in May, at a primary school somewhere in south-west England. What is going on?

Two girls from an Infants class are sitting on the grass making daisy chains –also using the odd buttercup.

Boys from a Juniors class are playing the Bench Game, a kind of Tag in which a playground bench is the base.

Several Infant girls have squeezed under a playground table, pretending it is a house.

Three Junior boys are kicking a football to one another. Nearby, some of their classmates are trading Pokémon cards.

Three more boys, this time from the Infants, are squatting on their haunches and jumping towards one another, each trying to make the others overbalance.

A group of four Infant girls is playing a clapping game and singing:

My boyfriend gave me an apple.
My boyfriend gave me a pear.
My boyfriend gave me a kiss on the lips.
And threw me down the stairs.

I gave him back his apple.
I gave him back his pear.
I gave him back his kiss on the lips.
And threw him down the stairs.

Lots of children, especially the younger ones, are chasing each other around, apparently aimlessly.

Four infant boys are playing an imaginary game of *Star Wars*, duelling with pretend light sabres.

A couple of children are playing with Diabolos.

Half a dozen Junior boys are taking part in a game called Dominoes in which they all squat down in a line next to each other and then the one at the end gives a shove so that they all push each other over in sequence like tumbling dominoes.

A group of girls and boys is performing handstands on the grass. Just before they put down their hands and kick up their heels, they say:

Under, over,
Pepsi Cola,
One, two, three.

Then the bell goes; time to go in.

Twenty Questions

Anyone's Guess

A traditional guessing game formerly much played at parties, Twenty Questions is now regarded as rather old-fashioned, which is a shame.

One player thinks of an object and tells the other players whether it is 'Animal', 'Vegetable' or 'Mineral'; 'Abstract' or 'Other' are additional categories that can be used. 'Animal' describes an object that is a member of the animal kingdom, 'Vegetable' an object derived from the plant kingdom, 'Mineral' anything geological in origin, and 'Abstract' or 'Other' denotes anything else. So a paper bag would be Vegetable as paper comes from trees, a stone would be Mineral, and a leather bag, Animal. Confused? Many were.

The other players have twenty questions between them with which to guess the object. Each question must be phrased so that a 'yes' or 'no' answer can be given.

For example, if the object in question is a tiger, it will be described as 'Animal'. Players might then pursue the following line of questioning:

'Is it alive?' – 'Yes'

'Is it a mammal?' – 'Yes'

'Is it a domestic animal?' – 'No'

'Is it a herbivore?' – 'No'

'Is is a carnivore?' – 'Yes'

'Is it found in Europe?' – 'No'

'Does it have fur?' – 'Yes'

'Is it a cat?' – 'Yes'

'Is it a lion?' – 'No'

Twenty Questions gave rise to a popular radio programme of the same name that was broadcast on BBC Radio 4 from the late 1940s until the mid 1970s. A typical list of objects to be guessed on the show would include such items as Bugs Bunny, malt whisky, a Scilly Isle, the complete works of Shakespeare and a wooden leg.

The categories of Animal, Vegetable and Mineral may have their origins in the Gilbert and Sullivan opera *The Pirates of Penzance* in which Major-General Stanley sings:

'I am the very model of a modern Major-General,
I've information vegetable, animal, and mineral,
I know the kings of England, and I quote the fights
    historical'

A version of Twenty Questions called 'Yes and No' is played by some of the characters in Charles Dickens' *A Christmas Carol*.

Twenty Questions is often played thematically, with players having to guess, for example, the name of a famous person, a place, an animal or an occupation ('zookeeper'). This last option inspired another popular radio show of the 1950s and 1960s entitled 'What's My Line?'.

Twenty Questions may seem rather pedestrian in these days of quick-fire quiz shows, but its vaguely scientific slant ('I didn't know a bin bag was mineral') gives it possibilities as an educational game. It is also a useful standby on a long car journey when everyone is bored with I Spy.

Wheelbarrow Race

Where Push Comes to Shove

Wheelbarrow racing is pretty gruelling, especially for the Wheelbarrow. Anyone game enough to participate needs a teammate. One forms the wheelbarrow by kneeling down with his hands on the ground. The other grabs hold of the Wheelbarrow's ankles or calves, holding them either side of his own body. The Wheelbarrow then walks along the ground by means of his hands, while his teammate walks behind him supporting his legs. It is possible to go quite quickly if partners work well in tandem, but barrow-collapse and tripping-up scenarios are common.

The usual way of organizing a wheelbarrow race is to have the competitors race to a line, and then swap positions for the return leg. Competitive wheelbarrow races are held in locations all over the country, often as charity events. Beer can be a driving factor in the antics, cut and bruised hands the invariable result.

If it all proves too much, you can always stick to gardening!

Wink Murder
Killing You Softly

Apopular party game, Wink Murder has the advantages of being played in relative quiet and of allowing those with acting talent to ham it up.

At least six players are needed for the game but there is no upper limit – the more the merrier. Everyone stands or sits in a circle. One player is chosen to be the Detective and leaves the room. One of the remaining players is selected to be the Murderer. Then the Detective comes back into the room and stands in the middle of the circle.

The Murderer 'kills' as many players as possible by winking at them, one by one. Once a player sees the Murderer wink, they must die. Blood-curdling screams and melodramatic or lingering death-throes are permissible, as are silent slumps to the floor. The Detective watches carefully and tries to catch the Murderer in the act. The Detective is allowed three guesses to the identity of the Murderer, but if they fail to guess correctly the Murderer becomes the Detective for the next round. Alternatively, the last person left alive wins and becomes the next Detective.

The Murderer should avoid killing off too many people too quickly, as this narrows down the list of suspects. Killing only the people standing opposite is also a giveaway. Equally, the potential victims should try not to stare too obviously in the Murderer's direction. One way of preventing this is for the Murderer's identity to be kept secret from all the other players. Either everyone in the circle shuts their eyes while an adult or non-playing person goes round the circle and taps their choice of Murderer on the back. Or everyone pulls a piece of paper out of a hat; only one piece of paper has the letter M written on it and the person who draws it is the Murderer.

An explosive variant on Wink Murder involves the secret selection of a Bomb as well as a Murderer. If the person chosen to be the Bomb is winked at, they detonate loudly, instantly killing the Murderer.

'Vampire Murder' introduces an element of contagion into the game. A Vampire is secretly selected who then bares their teeth at as many of the other players as possible to convert them into Vampires. Anyone who spots the bared fangs becomes a Vampire and can start teeth-baring themselves. At any time, a player who is not yet a Vampire can accuse another of being one by shouting 'Stake him!'. If they are correct, the Vampire dies and is out. The object of the game is to eliminate all the Vampires without being converted into one.

'Murder Handshake' makes it harder to identify the guilty party. Players move around the room shaking hands. The Murderer kills by using a special handshake, perhaps squeezing instead of shaking the hand, or scratching the victim's palm. In this version, all the players are the Detectives. Any player can make an accusation, but if they are wrong, they too must die.

Whichever version is played, it is all blinking good fun!

CRAZY FOR YOU
Playground Crazes

We all remember them, those fads for particular toys and games that punctuated our childhoods. They can even pinpoint how old we are. A former cigarette card-skimmer? You had a wartime boyhood. Remember Clackers? You were a 1970s girl. Tying yourself up in knots of Scoubidous? A child of the Noughties!

Crazes can take a feverish hold of a whole playground within weeks and then disappear as quickly as they arrived, leaving the object of desire abandoned at the back of cupboards – perhaps to be retrieved years later, either as a valuable antique or because, just like other fashions, crazes have a habit of coming around again: witness the recent fad for Diabolos, a toy thought to have originated in ancient China.

Clackers

Also known as 'Kernockers', Clackers were a craze of the early 1970s and consisted of two hard plastic balls on pieces of string, joined together by a ring. The idea was to hold the ring and swing the balls in such a way that you clacked them together quickly and as many times as possible without stopping. The balls could be clacked together in mid-air, or against the ground or wall. Clackers were banned in many schools as they were potentially lethal, particularly if they flew out of a player's hand mid-clack; bruised wrists, knuckles and even faces were common side-effects of this craze.

Rubik's Cube

This fiendish puzzle was invented in 1974 by a Hungarian sculptor and architecture professor called Erno Rubik. Each face of a Rubik's Cube is covered by nine squares, each in one of six different colours. The aim of the puzzle is to twist the top, bottom and side faces of the cube (all of which pivot) so that each face contains nine squares of the same colour. Homes and playgrounds in the early 1980s were full of people twisting away at their cubes, concentrating furiously and cursing a wrong move. After hours and hours of 'cubing', a few people did solve the puzzle, while others resorted to chiselling apart their cubes in frustration.

Trading Cards

Since cigarette cards first appeared in the late 19th century, collecting cards and swapping duplicates to make up sets or obtain particularly covetable cards has been an almost permanent craze, with only the type of card changing. Cigarette cards gave way after World War II to cards included in packets of tea and confectionery, a practice that continued until the 1970s and 1980s. Cards and medallions featuring pictures of endangered wildlife, football teams or other themes were also given away with the purchase of petrol. In more recent decades, sets that combine the universal childhood craze for collecting with a game, such as Pokémon and Match Attax, have become the cards of choice.

Hula Hoops

Inspired by the hoops with which children have played since ancient times, Hula Hoops were a plastic version patented in America in the 1950s. The gyrating Hawaiian dance contributed the 'Hula' part of the name because of its similarity to the movement that hoopers performed in their attempt to keep the hoop spinning around their midriff. Hula Hoops were an international craze in the 1950s, with 25 million sold worldwide in only four months. Concern was expressed in some countries, notably Japan and Russia, about the propriety of wiggling one's hips so suggestively while hooping. Although the craze waned in the 1960s, hooping has recently made a comeback after being widely publicized as excellent cardio-vascular exercise.

Scoubidous

Scoubidous have nothing to do with the similar-sounding Hanna Barbera cartoon featuring a band of pesky kids and their lily-livered mutt. They are hollow plastic tubes about 80 cm in length which come in a variety of colours and are plaited and knotted together to make objects such as key fobs, friendship bracelets, bookmarks and even little animals. The activity recalls macramé and even the ancient craft of making corn dollies, but is believed to have originated in France, where it was a huge craze in the 1950s and 1960s. In 1958, Sacha Distel scored his first hit record with a song called 'Scoubidou' and this is thought to be the origin of the name. Scoubidous only became a playground craze in the UK during the mid-Noughties, when even boys were swept up in it. Who would have thought plaiting could be so cool?

Yellow Car
I Saw It First!

Yellow Car can be played at any time and anywhere. In fact, Yellow Car is never not being played, as no warning of a game having started is necessary.

The game can be played outdoors or on a car journey. Players look out for yellow cars; lorries, taxis and other four-wheeled vehicles can be included at the players' discretion. When someone spots a yellow car, they are allowed to punch another player. If the spotter wishes, they can also shout 'Yellow car!'. However, in games in a car, the driver has immunity from punches, in the interests of safety!

Only cars that are yellow qualify; shades of gold and orange are not acceptable, and multi-coloured vehicles must be at least 50 per cent yellow to qualify. Ideally, the vehicle that has been spotted must be seen by at least one other player for the punch to be allowed, although in the case of twisty roads or motorways on which a car can disappear quickly, an element of trust is required. If a player hits someone else when no yellow car has been spotted, the recipient of the punch has the right to return the blow.

The same car cannot be 'spotted' twice, and cars do not count that can be guaranteed to be in a certain place, such

as a yellow car belonging to a neighbour or a yellow car in a local car showroom.

A common variation on the game allows two punches to be given for spotting a yellow Mini. If a non-violent version is preferred, spotters can simply shout out 'Yellow car, I win' when they spot a yellow car.

In a similar game called 'Punch Buggy', players spot VW Beetle cars. On sighting one, the spotter calls out 'Punch buggy red' or 'Punch buggy orange', depending on its colour, as they deliver the blow. Adding 'no punch back!' is also recommended, thus preventing the punchee from 'double spotting' the same vehicle. Purists restrict their Beetle spotting to models made before Volkswagen introduced the new-style Beetle in 1998, but for most people a Beetle is a Beetle. Mention should also be made of 'Pinch Mini' in which Minis and pinches are substituted for Beetles and punches.

The most exciting place in the world to play Yellow Car is New York City, although a fine set of bruises would be the probable result.

Bibliography

Bibliography

Kelleher, Susan (ed), *The Games We Played*, English Heritage, 2007

Opie, Iona and Peter, *Children's Games in Street and Playground*, Oxford University Press, 1969

Pick, J B, *The Phoenix Dictionary of Games*, Phoenix House Ltd, 1952

Roberts, Chris, *Heavy Words, Lightly Thrown: The Reason Behind the Rhyme*, Granta, 2004

Vivian, Mary, *Party Games for Children of All Ages*, Foulsham, 1940

Useful websites

www.bbc.co.uk/dna/h2g2 a BBC online encyclopaedia and community, with message boards featuring reminiscences about games played in childhood

www.gameskidsplay.net an American website dedicated to sharing information about children's games and rhymes

www.gamesmuseum.uwaterloo.ca the website of the Elliott Avedon Museum and Archive of Games at the University of Waterloo, Ontario, Canada

www.livingarchive.org.uk/hidden the website of a project carried out by Bushfield Middle School, Wolverton, Milton Keynes; features current playground games and rhymes

www.playgroundfun.org.uk a government-sponsored website featuring playground games and other ideas for play

www.streetplay.com an American website documenting street games

www.tradgames.org.uk a website providing information about the history and rules of traditional games

www.vam.ac.uk/moc the website of the V&A Museum of Childhood, Bethnal Green, London

www.woodlands-junior.kent.sch.uk the website of Woodlands Junior School, Tonbridge, Kent; features online educational and recreational games

Index of Game Names
and Variants

Index of Game Names and Variants

Games which have a main entry in this book are shown in bold type. Variant names are shown in roman.

Index of Game Names and Variants

Index of Game Names and Variants

Index of Game Names and Variants